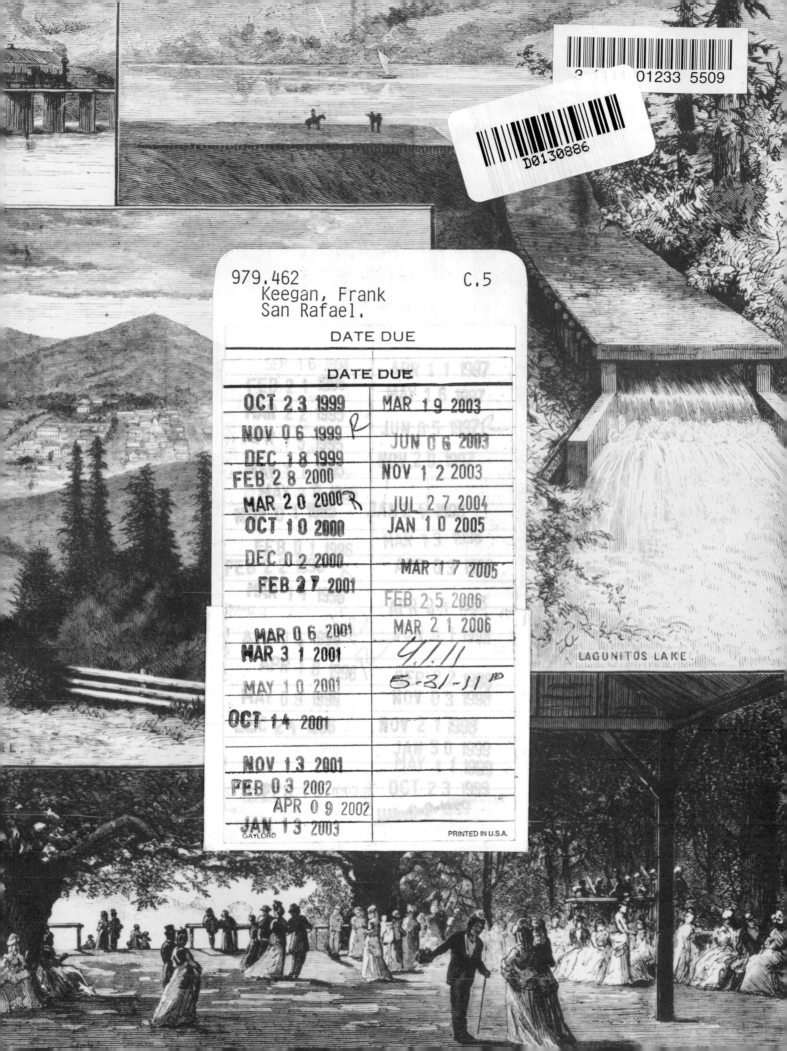

LAGUNITOS LAKE.

SAN RAFÆL
MARIN'S MISSION CITY

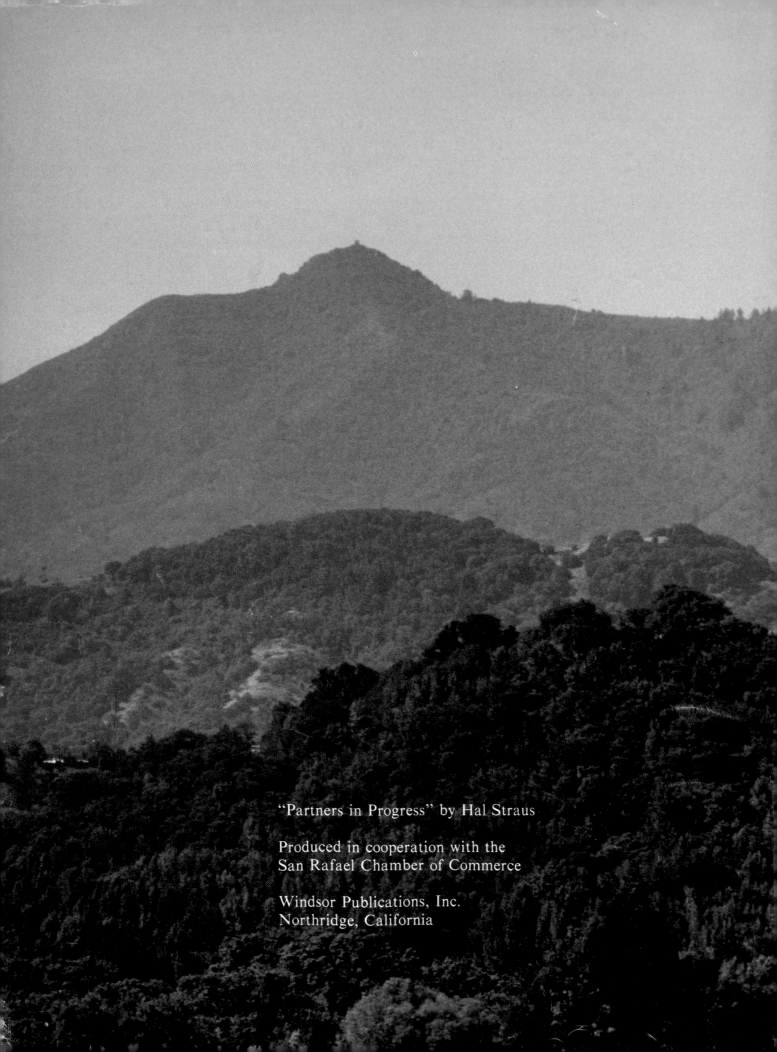

"Partners in Progress" by Hal Straus

Produced in cooperation with the
San Rafael Chamber of Commerce

Windsor Publications, Inc.
Northridge, California

SAN RAFÆL

MARIN'S MISSION CITY

An Illustrated History

by
FRANK L. KEEGAN

Windsor Publications, Inc.—History Book Division

Vice-President/Publishing: Hal Silverman
Editorial Director: Teri Davis Greenberg
Design Director: Alexander D'Anca
Corporate Biography Director: Karen Story

Staff for *San Rafael: Marin's Mission City*
Editor: Lane A. Powell
Assistant Director, Corporate Biographies: Phyllis Gray
Editor, Corporate Biographies: Brenda Berryhill
Production Editor, Corporate Biographies: Una FitzSimons
Editorial Assistants: Kathy M. Brown, Susan Kanga, Nina Kanga, Pat Pittman
Proofreader: Susan J. Muhler
Layout Artist, Corporate Biographies: Mari Catherine Preimesberger, Angela María Ortiz
Designer: Tanya Maiboroda

Library of Congress Cataloging-in-Publication Data

Keegan, Frank L.
　San Rafael: Marin's Mission City / by Frank L. Keegan.
Partners in Progress / by Hal Straus. — 1st ed.
　　p.　　cm.
　　"Produced in cooperation with the San Rafael Chamber of Commerce."
　　Bibliography: p.139
　　Includes index.
　　ISBN 0-89781-221-2
　　1. San Rafael (Calif.)—History. 2. San Rafael (Calif.)—Description. 3. San Rafael (Calif.)—Industries. I. Straus, Hal. Partners in progress. 1987. II. Title. III. Title: Partners in progress.
F869.S399K44　　1987
979.4'62—dc19　　　　　　　　　　87-18776CIP

To Frederick G. Knell, native of San Rafael,
Bookman and Friend

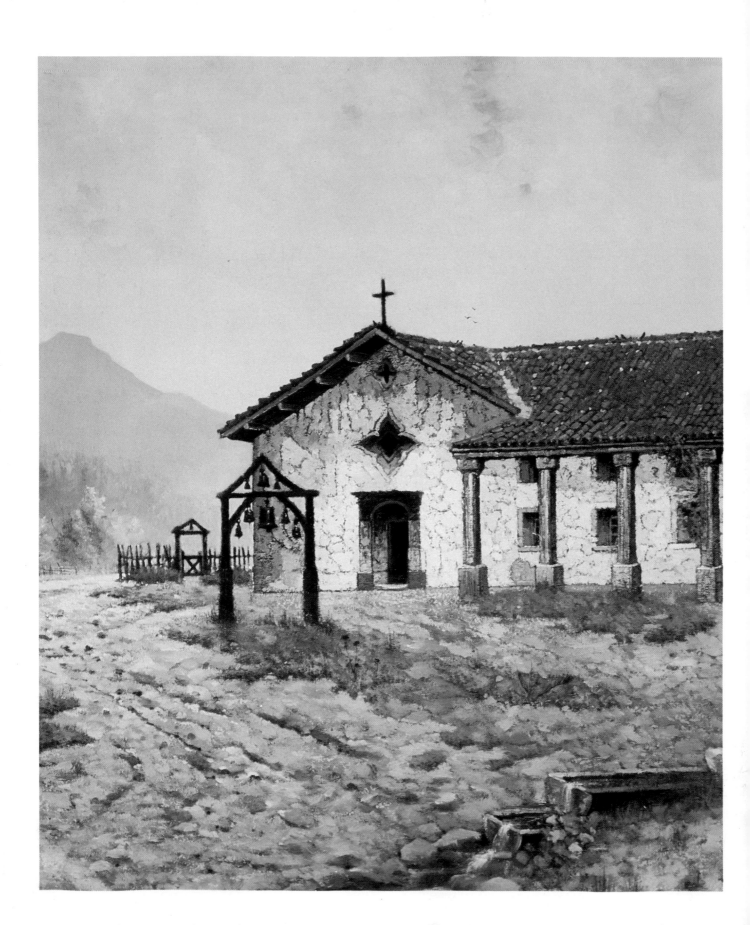

CONTENTS

ACKNOWLEDGMENTS

The preparation of a manuscript and the identification of images long past cannot be the work of a single person. Books may indeed be written by a single hand, but they reflect the work of many others. Jeanne M. Leoncini, San Rafael's city clerk, and John Dorich in the City Planning Office, helped me understand contemporary San Rafael, while Msgr. Thomas I. Kennedy, pastor of Saint Rafael's Church, kept the city's past vividly before me. Suzan Davis, executive director of the San Rafael Chamber of Commerce, was constantly helpful, and Dorothy Morgan, curator of the Marin County Historical Society, shared photographic treasures and put them in perspective. Michael Moore of the U.S. Geological Survey (Menlo Park) provided aerial photo assistance, and Roy Aker, historian and scholar, reviewed my text on the Spanish explorers of Marin. Arthur Quinn, an able author and historian, assisted by reviewing the entire manuscript.

Nan and Roy Farrington Jones of Ross opened their historical files and magnificent slide collection to me while Jocelyn A. Moss, librarian of the Ann T. Kent History Room of the Marin County Library, provided especially valuable assistance in identifying sources and sharing her own vast knowledge of San Rafael and Marin County.

Finally, my editor, Lane A. Powell, was a constant source of encouragement and good ideas. All writers need editors like Mr. Powell.

The Marin County Courthouse at the corner of Fourth and A streets was completed in March 1873. In this 1875 photo its towering cupola and landscaped gardens enclosed in a picket fence can be seen. Later the cupola was removed, yet the building remained for a century as the most imposing structure in San Rafael. On May 25, 1971, it was destroyed by fire, but by this time the Marin Civic Center had already been constructed and occupied. Courtesy, Bancroft Library

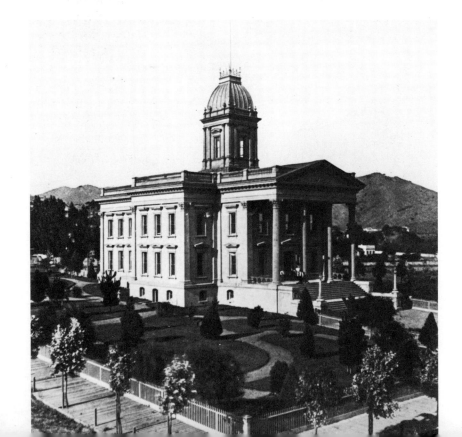

PREFACE

In any city on earth, you may look in four directions. What makes San Rafael unique is that any way you look the view is spectacular. Nestled securely in brown foothills amid the dark green, native oak, San Rafael looks east toward the morning sun rising over San Francisco Bay, north to the rolling hills and golden valleys of the wine country, west to the broad Pacific Ocean, and south to its mighty, solemn guardian, the sleeping Indian maiden, Mount Tamalpais.

Yet it is not the excellent scenery surrounding San Rafael, or that it is the heart, the center, the county seat of "Marvelous Marin," nor even that its historical roots go deeper than any of the other picturesque towns and hamlets on the Marin peninsula that makes the city distinctive. What makes San Rafael unique is that, for the parade of people who have dwelt here from earliest times, it has been a haven, a refuge, a retreat, a sanctuary, a home.

The area has attracted a colorful assortment of human beings, including Miwok man searching for a wider hunting ground, Spanish explorers seeking golden kingdoms, Yankee sea captains pursuing the great whale, Russian hunters killing sea otters for their pelts, Missouri mountain men avid for pleasure after long treks, Irish laborers building the railroads, Chinese fishermen netting shrimp, and American adventurers asserting Manifest Destiny. Many of the visitors became permanent residents, calling San Rafael their home.

The natural history of a city often explains its human history, and San Rafael is no exception. What its human inhabitants perceived as a safe haven had already been prepared by nature over millions of years. Whether one looks above the earth to half-mile high Mount Tamalpais or below the earth to geologic formations, nature anticipated man. Just as the mountain to the south protects San Rafael from damp coastal fogs pouring through the Golden Gate inundating San Francisco, so does the San Andreas fault obligingly run far to the west of San Rafael, giving the city immunity from the most severe natural disaster in California, the earthquake.

It seems that San Rafael has been crafted by a giant's benevolent hand, endowing it with what all its inhabitants have sought—protection. The Miwok Indians first discovered its hospitable hills and accessible bays and found a sanctuary thousands of years before Sir Francis Drake in the *Golden Hinde* sought safe anchorage in 1579 in the bay carved out by Point Reyes peninsula. About the time of the American Revolution, San Rafael was discovered by Spanish military officers as a sunny alternative to San Francisco. Early in the nineteenth century, the first Christian missionaries built a chapel and hospital amid its fog-free hills, while in the later part of the century wealthy San Franciscans enjoyed San Rafael as a resort and spa. In our own century, the city has provided refuge for San Francisco's homeless stricken by the Earthquake of 1906, and today thousands of people live and work here in preference to the overcrowded cities that ring the San Francisco Bay Area.

The story of San Rafael is the story of diverse peoples seeking protection and finding it. Whether as a haven or home—a refuge to escape disaster, a retreat and resort to replenish the spirit, or a sanctuary—San Rafael has proved hospitable to the many, varied people who have sought a better life here. The story of San Rafael is also the story of the historic mark each group has indelibly placed upon the city. In the pages that follow, both these stories will be told.

CHAPTER 1

THE ANCIENT LAND AND THE COYOTE PEOPLE

An aerial view of Marin County reveals not one, but two peninsulas. The larger one, the peninsula of Marin, runs north and south pointing toward the city of San Francisco. Creases in the eastern hills have allowed creeks to form, which flow into both the larger San Francisco Bay and the little bays shaped by fingers of land. The second, smaller peninsula, Point Reyes, points westward to the sea, facing the largest ocean in the world, the Pacific. Between them runs a deep cleavage in the earth, a rift valley, the pathway of the San Andreas fault.

The two peninsulas are the meeting place of the North American continent as it inches slowly westward and the northwesterly moving Pacific Plate emerging from the sea to glance off the continent. Geologically speaking, East meets West in Marin County. These two titans began their collision course about 30 million years ago and geologists estimate that in the next 30 million years San Francisco will be abreast of today's Seattle, Washington. The past 30 million years have created Marin's two peninsulas, two climates, and two earth zones.

The division between them is best seen at Tomales Bay, which has been called "Earthquake Bay," because the San Andreas fault lies directly beneath its shallow waters. Earthquakes are common in California and each slight tremor records the almost imperceptible movement of the North American Plate rubbing shoulders with the Pacific Plate. This abrasive encounter is revealed in dramatic fashion in Marin County's two peninsulas.

Though difficult to believe today, California was once tropical with huge marshes and inlets that allowed a rich growth of plants and trees. Fossil remains reveal that about 15 million years ago the marshes of Marin held willow trees and swamp cypress, much like Florida's Everglades today, along with cherry, alder, sycamore, and poplar trees. Later, in the Pleistocene epoch (1-3 million years ago), the Sequoia Redwood was indigenous to northern California.

Facing page: Members of the Tcholovoni tribe hunted with bows and arrows on the edge of San Francisco Bay. Their quivers were cases made from the skins of sea otters. Early Russian explorers noted that not all the Indian tribes hunted. Marin's coastal Miwok Indians, who admired the cunning of the coyote, told tales of how he created the world and Man. Courtesy, Bancroft Library

Above: A drawing of the Marin peninsula shows the outline of Point Reyes as similar to the shape of the head of a coyote. Note the blunt nose of the peninsula adjacent to an open mouth, which is Drake's Bay. An eye and an ear may also be discovered.

Ancient animals also roamed Marin's hills and valleys, almost matching the mighty redwoods in size and power. These huge mammals included the mammoth tusked elephant, giant ground sloths, horses, camels, giant jaguars, great wolves, and bison. Perhaps the most fearsome of all was the saber-toothed tiger, called Smilidon, the official state fossil of California. The Muir Woods, Marin's own redwood forest, named for the great naturalist, John Muir, was home to these magnificent mammals. And just as the dinosaur before them vanished from the earth in a far earlier time, these animals also vanished from tropical California when the Pleistocene epoch ended.

The face of early man is obscure to us, and we learn of him only by the remains he left behind. Much of what we know is part fact and part conjecture, but as we move toward the present his face becomes more vivid and personal. Indeed, it is widely believed that the county of Marin itself is named for a particular Miwok Indian.

Anthropologists believe that man's first appearance on the North American continent coincided with the last of the several Ice Ages. Great sheets of ice moved down from the Arctic, which twisted and carved the Sierra Nevadas and the Rockies, dipping deep into

what is now Yosemite Valley, constructing massive art objects like Half Dome.

About 10,000 years ago, just before the last wall of ice retreated to the north, a land bridge across the Bering Sea between present-day Alaska and Russia permitted passage eastward for Siberian tribes. Slowly, over thousands of years, these hunter folk

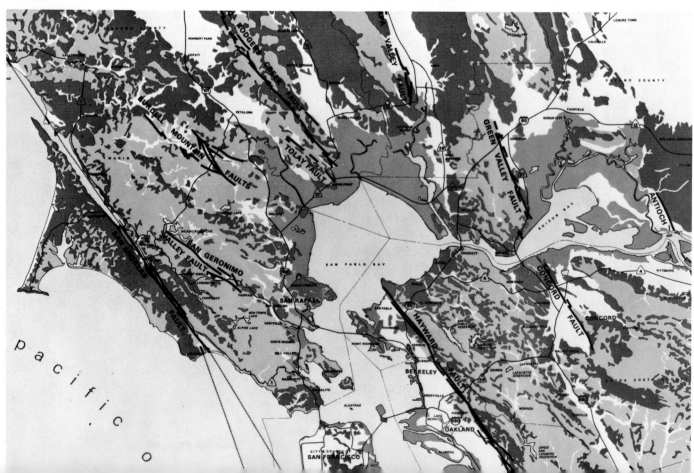

moved south and east toward warmer climates where game abounded. In northern California—just opposite present-day Richmond across the bay from San Rafael—shell mounds indicate that Indians were living here 4,500 years ago. Hundreds of these mounds, like so many ancient garbage heaps, dot the shores of San Francisco Bay, suggesting how habitable these lands and waters were.

The face of Marin County's Indians was defined most sharply in June 1579 when Sir Francis Drake's *Golden Hinde* sought safe harbor within the bay created by the Point Reyes peninsula, the bay now known as Drake's Bay. His chaplain, Francis Fletcher, described the people who met him as

having a tractable, free and loving nature, without guile or treachery . . . the men commonly (are) so strong of body that that which 2 or 3 of our men could hardly beare, one of them would take upon his back and without grudging carrie it easily away, up hill and downe hill an English mile together . . . Their men for the most part goe naked; the women take a kinde of bulrushes . . . make themselves thereby a loose garment . . . which . . . hanges downe about their hippes, and so affordes to them a covering of that which nature teaches should be hidden.

The first effort of Drake and his men was to clothe the Indians, suggesting the pattern of enforced behavior that future centuries would witness between the Christian European and what we now know as the

Coastal Miwok people. The dominant civilization thus began the process that would ultimately destroy the native culture without successfully substituting its own.

Recent archeological research indicates that the Miwok people lived in over a dozen sites on the Marin peninsula, with the name *Awani-wi* given to the San Rafael area. They were divided into hunter-gatherers and fisher-foragers; the former roamed the hills and uplands while the latter, making light boats from tule

---

Facing page, top: This aerial photo (facing northwest) shows the San Andreas fault in Marin County stretching from Bolinas Bay in the foreground to Tomales Bay at top. To the left is the Point Reyes peninsula composed of igneous rock and granite, among the hardest stone in existence. To the right is the Marin peninsula, composed of sedimentary rock, shale, and sandstone. Photo by Robert E. Wallace. Courtesy, U.S. Geological Survey

Facing page, bottom: This map illustrates why San Rafael escaped the destruction that the 1906 earthquake wreaked upon San Francisco. San Rafael lay far enough east of the San Andreas fault to have escaped most effects. Courtesy, U.S. Geological Survey

Above: Charles R. Knight's mural depicts a huge ground sloth, saber-toothed tigers, giant vultures, and giant wolves. Mammoth elephants (or mastodons) and bisons are seen in the background. Fossil remains of these ancient animals were found in the Rancho La Brea tar pits in Los Angeles. Paleontologists agree that similar creatures roamed Marin County in prehistoric times. Courtesy, Los Angeles County Museum of Natural History

reeds, paddled in the bays and estuaries. Their lives were built around clans or small communities often named for an animal spirit, and were regulated by the seasons, the growth and flowering of plants, the spawning of the salmon, the migration of birds.

The staple Miwok food was an acorn meal. Women and children would gather the acorns and husk and grind them into a paste with a stone mortar and pestle. They would then pour boiling water over the paste to leach out the bitter, tannic taste. From the acorn meal, cakes or mush could be prepared to be eaten or to be stored for food during the long winter. Other plants and flowers were known to the Miwok women, who spent years learning the applications of growing things for food, medicine, and other practical uses. Rudimentary agricultural methods, like burning grass to bring forth new shoots, were employed, but planting seed was unknown.

The diet of the Miwok was ample and varied, and included clams, mussels, and abalone along with fish, birds, rabbits, squirrels, deer, and bear. Only a few animals, such as the skunk and snake, were not eaten. Fish were caught in nets or speared, while ducks were trapped by nets strung between patches of tules. The Miwok never killed all he captured, leaving always some prey to escape, for he knew his survival depended upon theirs. They trod lightly on the land, their footsteps barely visible.

The Miwoks were animists and believed that animals and men had a common ancestry. Before killing deer, apologies were made to the stricken animals, and hunters danced under the hide and antlers to give themselves the power of the animal's spirit. Dancing was common, either by special dancers in secret societies or by the people themselves to celebrate a kill or special harvest.

Commerce between tribes was effected through the exchange of clam-shell beads for desirable objects, such as the black obsidian used to make arrow points, which the Miwok procured from the Pomo Indians to the north. Territories were clearly defined and the pursuit of game or other intrusion of a clan into another's land required payment either in the form of beads or perhaps part of the kill. There is little evidence of war and raiding between tribes, and then only for the infringement of territorial rights.

Without a written language, the Miwok and neighboring Pomo spoke most eloquently in the sophisticated, elaborately woven basketry. Tightly woven, the baskets could hold water. The designs, colors, and shapes are extraordinary and only among these tribes, in all of California, did men also have a share in basket making. The most intricate work, however, was done by women. A.L. Kroeber has noted, "Their general disposition of patterns on the surface of baskets displays a greater variety than is found elsewhere . . . the art of basketry in all its phases underwent an independent, special and uncommon development." Many of the most beautiful of Miwok and Pomo baskets were placed upon the funeral pyres of the dead, and were destroyed with them.

The Indians' culture was transmitted through the songs and dances of the shaman and through stories told in the sweat houses. Built by excavation, with rounded domes of earth and redwood construction, the sweat houses were the social centers of male Miwok life. Inside was a fire pit producing intense heat that only the strongest could withstand. A clean people, often bathing twice daily, the Miwok knew that human scent could be detected by the animals he hunted and, for this reason, the hunters carefully scraped themselves clean in the sweat houses before the hunt began.

Whether by their preparation for deer hunting on the hillsides, or by the construction of tule-reed boats for netting salmon on the bays, the Miwok on the Marin peninsula achieved an almost perfect harmony between their ways and the bounty of nature. Even the face of the earth itself seemed to reflect this unity, for even a casual glance at the county's outline, with its two peninsulas, suggests the native dog, the coyote. With the head turned to the sea, Tomales Bay serving as a drooping ear, and the estuaries of Drake's Bay defining the mouth, the land itself spoke of what the Miwok people called Coyote Man, the creator of the world.

The young Miwok male in the sweat house would hear the tale of how man was made. He would hear the shaman and the older men tell how the coyote, after creating the world, summoned all the animals to discuss the creation of man. Placing the mighty grizzly bear on his right and all the animals around him in a circle, with the lowly mouse on his left, the coyote asked each animal to speak. Each responded by proposing that man should have his particular feature: the mountain lion's roar, the elk's antlers, the grizzly's strength, and so on through them all.

Coyote spoke last, upbraiding the other animals for their self-gratification. Coyote knew he was not the best of animals that one could conceive and the chal-

Facing page: Juan Rodriguez Cabrillo sailed down the California coast in 1542 in the San Salvador *and the* Victoria. *Though Cabrillo died during his voyage, he is credited with the discovery of upper California and the exploration of much of the coast. Courtesy, National Park Service*

Above: This scene depicts Miwok Indians crowning Sir Francis Drake king after he landed near Point Reyes peninsula in today's Marin County in 1579. Note the ships in the background and soldiers planting a plate of brass announcing England's acquisition of California. The painting by John de Bry, a contemporary of Drake, shows the men as naked and the women as partly clothed. Two hundred years later, Spanish missionaries would try to teach Christian modesty to the Miwok Indians. Courtesy, Bancroft Library

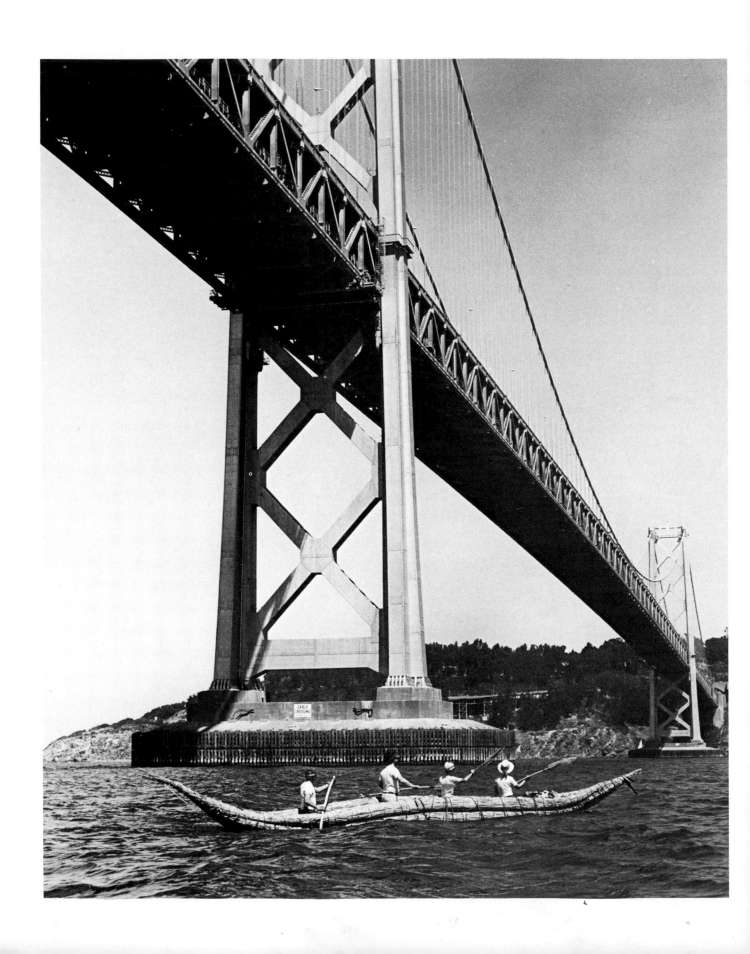

lenge was to make man the best animal possible. He admitted that the lion's roar could frighten, the antlers of the elk were beautiful, the grizzly was powerful, the lack of fur on the fish helped him swim, and that the eagle's grasping claw was useful. Yet, said the coyote, no one but he could give man wit and cunning.

The other animals roared their disapproval and wrangled with one another over the creation of man. Finally, each animal set to work to construct man according to his own idea of what man should be like. But it became late and each one slowly fell asleep, leaving the coyote to work through the night and complete his model. He then discharged water on each of the other models, destroying them. By morning's first light, he breathed life into his work before the other animals awoke. And so was man made by the coyote.

So, long before Charles Darwin, the legend reveals the Miwok belief in the common ancestry of men and animals. With each animal man shares a special feature, including the cunning of the coyote. The Miwok never forgot his spiritual lineage in dealing with living things. Arthur Quinn illustrates in his book, *Broken Shore,* that here on the Marin peninsula the powerful unity between men and animals is embodied in the very earth, giving the image of the coyote to the jutting land pointing eastward to the sea.

The story of Coyote Man was carried deep within the Miwok and was passed from one generation to another, until the white man came.

Facing page: Against the towering background of the San Francisco-Oakland Bay Bridge, four modern naturalists in 1979 paddle a reconstruction of an Indian tule-reed canoe. They described it as a "floating sofa," easily navigated in either deep water or the shallow estuaries of San Francisco Bay. Courtesy, East Bay Regional Park Service

Below: This 1816 drawing portrays Indians on San Francisco Bay using double-bladed paddles to convey a tule-reed canoe over the choppy waters. The tule reed was abundant in bay waters along the shore. The artist, Ludovic Choris, was an illustrator on a Russian exploratory voyage to San Francisco Bay. Courtesy, Bancroft Library

THE EUROPEAN EXPLORERS

The story of San Rafael is first the story of the discovery of California. While it is clear enough that Englishman Francis Drake was the first European to set foot on California's Marin County, his step was so light that historians still debate the exact place where he trod. It is quite the opposite with the subsequent Spanish explorers, for their pathways in California are long, rich and enduring.

The search for California began in Spain with the publication of a late-fifteenth-century novel. Written by Ordonez de Montalvo, *The Exploits of Esplandian* is a romance of chivalry well known to those who are familiar with the adventures of King Arthur and Don Quixote. It was Ordonez who first linked California with gold:

Know ye that at the right hand of the Indies is an island named California, very close to that part of the Terrestrial Paradise, which was inhabited by black women, without a single man among them, and they lived in the manner of Amazons . . . The island everywhere abounds with gold and precious stones . . . And there ruled over this island of California a queen of majestic proportions more beautiful than all the others, and in the very vigor of her womanhood.

The Amazon queen was named "Califia" and her story reached the heights of popularity through its publication on a Gutenberg press with movable type at about the time Hernando Cortes defeated the Aztec King, Montezuma, and conquered the magnificent city of Tenochtitlan in 1519-1521. After the conquest, Cortes wrote the Spanish ruler, Charles V, that he had heard of "an island of Amazons or women only, abounding in pearls and gold," not far from today's Baja California.

Facing page: Gaspar de Portola, the Spanish governor of Baja California, discovered San Francisco Bay in 1769. From bases in Lower California, Portola led an expedition northward to search for Monterey Bay. Unable to locate it using the 1603 description of Sebastian Vizcaino, Portola and his men, desperately short of food and water, pushed beyond today's Half Moon Bay to the mountains overlooking San Francisco Bay before returning south to San Diego. Drawing by Walter Francis. Courtesy, Bancroft Library

Above: Sir Francis Drake served his apprenticeship under John Hawkins, his cousin, and rose to become the most successful of all English sea captains in seizing Spanish booty and destroying Spanish vessels. He has been described as "one who commands and governs imperiously: sharp, ruthless, well-spoken, inclined to liberality and to ambition, boastful, not very cruel." Drake is regarded as the founder of the British maritime tradition. Courtesy, Bancroft Library

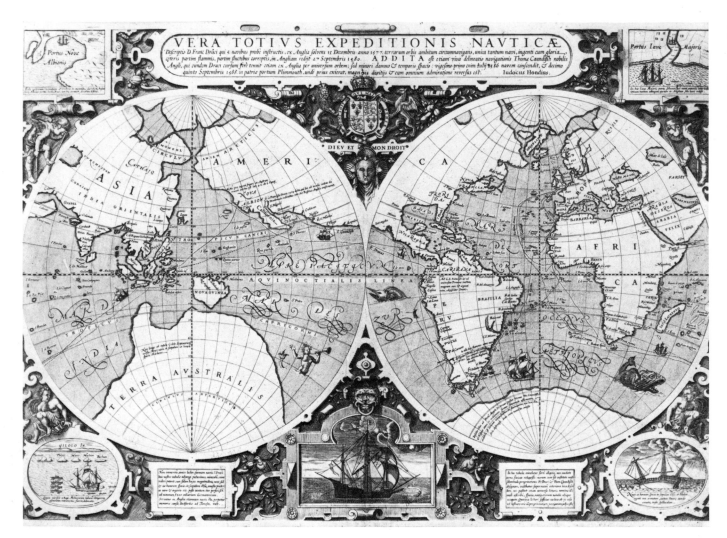

Mythical islands in romantic novels were not the only source of the Spanish ambition to reach the fabled Indies; there were also legends. The Seven Cities of Cibola, each founded by a Spanish bishop driven out of Spain by the Moors in the eighth century, were rumored to be vast storehouses of great wealth. The kingdom of La Gran Quivira contained kitchen utensils of pure gold. The Strait of Anian not only led to the Orient, but was lined with golden cities. Perhaps the most persistent myth concerned El Dorado, the man who was covered with gold every morning, then washed clean every evening, an act repeated daily.

Beyond the fiction, there were facts. Marco Polo had traveled to Cathay and Cipango (Japan) in the thirteenth century; the Portuguese had established the spice and silk trade with the Indies by traveling eastward; Columbus had mined gold in Cuba and Hispanola, present-day Haiti and the Dominican Republic, and Cortes himself had found rich stores of gold and

silver in the palaces of Montezuma. And while the Spaniards could not have known that Columbus' fourth voyage in 1502 had brought him but a few miles inland from the Pacific Ocean, just off the coast of present-day Honduras, they learned from Vasco Nunez de Balboa in 1513 of "the great mayne sea heretofore unknowen," which he named the Pacific.

All this knowledge, including the recent (1520-1521) circumnavigation of the globe by the Magellan expedition (also in Spain's service) was available to Hernando Cortes and his king, Charles V.

The exploits of Cortes have often been limited to his conquest of Mexico, with little regard for the almost 20-year period he spent exploring not only Mexico but Central America and Baja California as well. He was not only searching for a sea route to the Indies, as was Columbus, but for a northern passage to the riches of the Orient. Earlier explorations had shown that the way through the southern seas and around

Cape Horn were long and perilous. If a route lay open at latitudes shared by Europe, the path of exploration must lie to the north.

It is no exaggeration to say that the Spanish search for the Strait of Anian, or what was later called the "Northwest Passage," resulted in the discovery of California.

This brief survey cannot take account of the many efforts of the Spanish in the first half of the sixteenth century to explore both the land and sea in the territory known as New Spain. Soldiers like Francisco Vasquez de Coronado in 1540 searched the southwest as far as Kansas for the Seven Cities of Cibola, and mariners like Ulloa in 1539 and Cabrillo in 1542 sought the Strait of Anian. While they failed in their search, the name of Coronado endures as one of the most redoubtable land explorers of the West, Ulloa was the first to round the peninsula of Baja California, and Cabrillo is recognized as the discoverer of San Diego Bay, and his expedition probably sailed as far north as Cape Mendocino.

The explorations from New Spain were matched by others from Old Spain. After Magellan's discovery in 1521 of the Philippine Islands, other expeditions settled the islands and built from their shady trees the huge galleons that inaugurated the Spanish spice and silk trade with China and Japan. Annually, a huge galleon, capable of holding 300 tons, sailed westward from Mexico's west coast to the Orient, returning eastward to the California coast near Point Mendocino, then south to the port of Acapulco for overland passage of its cargo to the Caribbean and finally to Spain.

Near the end of the sixteenth century, two particular voyages—one English, the other Spanish—served to further define the part of California we now know as Marin County. The purpose of one mariner, Sebastian Rodriquez Cermenho, was to discover a northern California harbor suitable for the galleons returning fully laden with treasures from the Orient, while the purpose of the other sea captain, Francis Drake, was to relieve them of their burden.

Francis Drake had served his apprenticeship under John Hawkins in the Caribbean where he made a number of successful forays against the Spanish in Hispanola and along the Panamanian coast. Yet he yearned to carry his pursuits to the very heart of the growing Spanish empire, the Pacific trade route to the Indies.

Drake's famous voyage began in 1577, taking him

through the Strait of Magellan into the Pacific where he attacked both coastal settlements and ships at sea up the Peruvian and Mexican coasts. After taking much booty, heavily laden with Spanish treasure, he pointed his ship, the *Golden Hinde,* north toward the California coast.

In a sense, Drake had nowhere else to go. Behind him was an aroused Spanish population and before him the possibility of discovering the fabled Strait of Anian. The old ambition to reach the Orient had been achieved; what now was required was the shortest route there, one which the Spanish did not know. To discover a faster sea route to China and Japan would,

Facing page: The Flemish map-maker Hondius drew these spheres in 1590 showing the known world and the sea routes of Sir Francis Drake and his fellow Englishman, Thomas Cavendish, in their voyages around the world. Drake completed his voyage in 1580 and Cavendish in 1588. Note the drawing in the upper left-hand corner showing the "Port of Nova Albion" named by Francis Drake, at today's Point Reyes, Marin County. Though Ferdinand Magellan's ship, the Victoria, was the first vessel (1520) to circumnavigate the globe, Magellan himself was killed in the Moluccas and did not complete the voyage. Thus, Drake was the first captain to complete a circumnavigation of the globe and Cavendish the second. Courtesy, Bancroft Library

Above: This drawing depicts Sir Francis Drake's ship, the Golden Hinde, *rounding the tip of Point Reyes on June 17, 1579. Drake's voyage was the first European entry into California. Drake named these shores "Nova Albion" in honor of his English homeland. From this point, Drake headed due west, arriving in 1580 in Plymouth, England, becoming the first sea captain to circumnavigate the globe. Watercolor by Raymond Aker. Courtesy, Raymond Aker*

in effect, deprive the Spanish of their exclusive access to the Orient trade.

On June 17, 1579, Drake saw the chalky cliffs of California that were similar enough to the cliffs of Dover for him to name the new land "Nova Albion," from Britain's ancient Celtic title. And while debate occasionally arises on the precise place where he landed—Bolinas, Tomales Bay, and San Quentin Point all have their advocates—there is little doubt Drake landed in Marin County, with most experts and scholars concluding that the white cliffs he saw are the ones that stand today in the bay carved by Point Reyes, known today as Drake's Bay.

Drake himself commemorated the visit with a solemn proclamation claiming "Nova Albion" as part of England under Queen Elizabeth, and left a brass plate as evidence of the new acquisition. After spending almost six weeks refitting his ship, securing food and water, and after several peaceful encounters with the Coastal Miwok people, Drake headed west, landing in Plymouth, England, in 1580 to complete the circumnavigation of the globe. His success led many to conclude that he had indeed discovered the Strait of Anian.

The second voyage of discovery for Marin county began in 1595 under Sebastian Rodriquez Cermenho, a Portuguese navigator sailing for Spain. Leaving Manila on the *San Agustin*, he headed eastward toward the California coast with instructions to discover a harbor in which to land after the long, cruel passage from the Orient, a journey often taking six to eight months. Near the end of the eastern leg of this voyage,

the crews were but half-alive, with provisions low and disease rampant. The silks, spices, and porcelain crowded men above and below decks, while Pacific storms and unrelenting heat combined to produce conditions that imperiled both men and cargo. The need for a way station on the northern California coast was imperative and Cermenho, like Drake before him, found one.

It was the same bay under the arm of land we now know as Point Reyes, and Cermenho called it San Francisco Bay (Bahia de San Francisco). Like Drake, he explored the countryside and encountered the Miwok Indians, though they were less friendly and, indeed, hostilities broke out at one point. He, too, took possession of the land, this time in the name of the Spanish crown. It was the second foreign flag planted on Marin County's soil and was destined to have a much longer history than the first.

In his voyage from the Orient, Cermenho had the foresight to take aboard as deck cargo a pre-fabricated launch from the Philippines. While anchored off Point Reyes, his men had taken it off the *San Agustin* to assemble it for exploration along the coast when a heavy storm struck. The ship was pushed and battered against the shore, and the cargo and supplies were destroyed. It was the first recorded shipwreck on the California coast. Fortunately for Cermenho and his men, the launch survived, and they were lucky, indeed, in a magnificent exhibition of seamanship, to reach Acapulco after a voyage of 1,500 miles.

In retrospect it is not surprising that Marin County was discovered almost two centuries before San Francisco Bay, for the outer coast of California was the very boundary of the Spanish trade route with the Orient from 1565 to 1815. The earliest voyagers, like Drake and Cabrillo, came very close to the Bay's entrance, Drake stopping at the Farallone Islands for seal meat and gull's eggs. The frequent, if not perennial, fog disguised what we now know as the Golden Gate, and some voyagers passing along the coast were too far offshore to see it.

The search for a suitable California port for the Spanish galleons continued into the early seventeenth century with the 1602 voyage of Sebastian Rodriquez Vizcaino. Vizcaino's reputation is secure largely be-

cause of his success in charting the coastline and in the names he bestowed, which endure to the present day, including Santa Catalina Islands, Santa Barbara Islands, Santa Lucia Mountains and Point Reyes, the latter because he touched briefly at Drake's Bay on the Feast of the Three Kings (Tres Reyes), January 6, 1603.

Vizcaino is also remembered for his discovery of Monterey Bay, which he also named, though Cermenho may have seen it seven years earlier. Yet the name of Vizcaino is forever associated with Monterey Bay because his description of it confused all future travelers. He noted: "In addition to being so well situated in point of latitude for that which His Majesty intends to do for the protection and security of ships coming from the Philipines . . . the harbor is very secure against all winds." Whatever one may think of the

long, rounded bay at Monterey, its flat and treeless shore affords little protection from the wind.

Vizcaino's voyage ended for a time the exploration of northern California and it remained undisturbed for over a hundred and fifty years. In these years Spain was more than occupied with its European wars—in the seventeenth century with France and in the eighteenth century with England—coupled with periodic financial crises which even its rich trade with the colonies could not prevent. But if California slumbered, commercial activities continued throughout the Caribbean, New Spain, and Baja California, where the silver mines of Mexico and the continuing trade with the Orient occupied the full attention of the Spanish.

With the appointment in 1765 of Jose de Galvez as a specially appointed Inspector-General in New Spain, the colonization of California began. Galvez' presence signaled a change of policy. California, the largely unexplored land north of New Spain, was to be changed from unknown frontier to the status of a full colony. The reasons were political as well as economic, for a more formidable Spanish power was required to head off the Russians who had by that time settled the Aleutian Islands and were moving steadily southward in pursuit of the pelts of the sea otter and imperialistic expansion. In addition, the English, just concluding the Seven Years' War with France, had been ceded Canada by the Treaty of Paris (1763) and now had borders contiguous with New Spain.

If the earlier explorations of California and its coast had been successful as much by accident and mere chance as by design, the new Spanish explorations in eighteenth-century California were carefully planned to produce expected results.

Spain's purpose in the New World had always been twofold: to enrich the Empire and to save heathen souls. In the colonization of California these aims would be coordinated in a remarkable manner through the development of the missions. Missions have a long history in the Spanish records of the New World, for after the conquests and discoveries, Indians were often forcibly enrolled in settlements and given the tasks of farming, mining, hunting, and fishing. Whether directed by Jesuits, Dominicans, or Franciscans, missions were a distinct part of these settlements, the places where conversions were recorded and the sacraments conferred.

In 1767, two years after Galvez arrived in Mexico City, Spain suppressed the Jesuits, opening the way

for the Franciscans to replace them in the New World. The Franciscans responded enthusiastically to the new mandate and became the spiritual fathers to the California Indians in this still largely unexplored land. And it is to the land, not the sea, that we must now turn for the new phase of exploration which resulted in the discovery of San Francisco Bay.

The Spaniards planned a northern expedition to occupy and settle the harbors already known at San Diego and Monterey. Sea and land parties were organized under the command of the governor of Baja California, Gaspar de Portola, and the direction of the missions fell to the newly arrived Father Junipero Serra. The undertaking was ambitious. From tiny bases in Baja California—Cabo San Lucas and La Paz—the sea voyagers faced adverse winds while those heading north by land encountered parched deserts and arid plains.

Portola and Father Serra reached San Diego in 1769 and established a mission, with Father Serra remaining. Portola and Serra's friend, Father Juan Crespi, continued to head north. They reached the Salinas River and saw Monterey Bay, yet, because of Vizcaino's earlier description, failed to identify it. Indeed this error proved beneficial, for, after consultation with his men, Portola decided to push on in an effort to locate Monterey Bay.

It was in this final surge that the half-starved men, weary and ill, came upon Half Moon Bay, climbed a promontory of the Montara Mountains and saw the great bay we now know as San Francisco Bay. It was October 31, 1769. Ironically, Portola's diary contains the entry, "(we) have found nothing." What he meant was that in his search for Monterey Bay, he had seen "nothing" of it. Portola's failure to locate Monterey Bay was corrected a few months later after he and his men, along with Father Crespi, had returned from San Diego. Again sailing northward from San Diego he entered Monterey Bay on May 24, 1770, the bay Vizcaino had first discovered 168 years before. What Portola could not have known was that he had actually discovered something far greater, the harbor that would make possible the colonization of California—San Francisco Bay.

Even in that time, Portola's expedition was a success, for the rediscoverey of Monterey Bay became an important factor in further northern exploration. Supplied by San Diego to the south, Monterey Bay became an outpost both for land and sea journeys into Alta California. The names of Pedro Fages and Juan Bautista de Anza were among those who seized the opportunity by land, exploring beyond the bay to present-day Berkeley, Oakland, and the Carquinez Strait. Yet the approach by water awaited 1775, one year before the start of the American Revolution in the thirteen eastern seaboard colonies.

In the spring of 1775, a young Spanish captain and soldier, Juan Miguel de Ayala, was given orders to enter and explore the waters of San Francisco Bay. Leaving Monterey on July 27th, he set sail in the *San Carlos*, arriving at the entrance to the bay nine days later.

Ayala's logs and maps, and the diary of Father Vicente Santa Maria, the chaplain, reveal that they ventured to every part of the bay, marking with special care the northern portions, including Richardson Bay, San Pablo Bay, Carquinez Strait, Richmond, and Angel Island (which they named "Santa Maria de los Angeles"). There is little doubt the Spanish were, for the first time in almost 200 years, viewing Marin County, this time from its eastern shore.

The diary of Father Santa Maria recounts his visits with the Miwok Indians, the exchange of gifts, the invitation to visit their villages, and the first efforts at conversion. Both Santa Maria and Ayala were impressed with the "civilized bearing" of the Miwoks, the modesty of the women, their eagerness to repeat the Spanish prayers and make the Sign of the Cross. They exchanged songs and, for the first time, the sounds of Spanish and Latin mingled with the Miwok tongue. From that moment on, both the ancient land and the coyote man would be forever changed.

Ayala and Santa Maria, the soldier and the priest, together discovered the hills and valleys that now hold the city of San Rafael. Each was elated over his good fortune, with Ayala noting, "The harbor of San Francisco is one of the best I have seen in these seas, from Cape Horn northward," while Santa Maria wrote, "What is certain is that [the Indians] themselves seem to be asking a start at entering the fold of our Catholic religion. Not to avail of this opportunity would be a

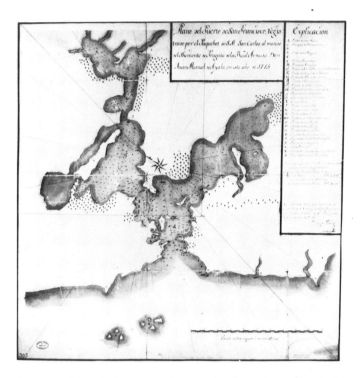

lamentable misfortune. To succeed as planned would be the best fortune of all."

Exploration and the spread of Christianity, never separate in the Spanish mind, were now joined on the shores of San Francisco Bay. What remained was the establishment of the presidios and missions to consolidate the successes of the several expeditions of the past few years, from Portola to Ayala. The modern history of northern California, and of San Rafael, had begun.

On August 5, 1775, the San Carlos, *the vessel of the young Spanish sea captain Juan Bautista de Ayala, became the first ship to enter San Francisco Bay—one year before the start of America's Revolutionary War. With the land route already opened up by Gaspar de Portola, Ayala's successful entry by water enabled the Spanish to extend their colonization into northern California. In his report Ayala noted that this bay "was the best we have seen in these seas from Cape Horn north, not one port only but many with a single entrance." Drawing by Walter Francis. Courtesy, Bancroft Library*

Above: This first map of San Francisco Bay shows several features quite clearly, like Angel Island and Yerba Buena (Treasure Island). The dark area is the outline of the bay waters and the white area represents the land. The map was probably drawn by Jose Canizares, the surveyor on board Juan de Ayala's vessel, the San Carlos. *In his longboat, Canizares spent many weeks taking soundings and naming geographical points as far as the mouth of the San Joaquin River. The map was registered in Mexico City on November 30, 1775. Courtesy, Bancroft Library*

CHAPTER 3

MISSION SAN RAFAEL ARCANGEL

In 1775, when Juan de Ayala first entered San Francisco Bay, a visitor whose presence was even more important for the founding of the Mission San Rafael arrived on the same shore. It was the indomitable President of the California missions, Father Junipero Serra.

Serra was now a man of 62 years of age who had seen the establishment of five missions, beginning with San Diego de Alcala a short six years before. With San Diego in the south and now San Francisco to the north, he confidently expected that many missions would be built throughout the entire California frontier. Like a holy necklace, the missions would grace the length and breadth of this new land, each link providing assistance to the next in time of need.

It was not merely a grand conception, but one which, by his death in 1784, he would see achieved in the formation of nine missions. In 1775, he would pause at the edge of the water and, looking north to the Marin hills, say, "Thanks be to God! Our Father Francis with the Holy Cross of the mission procession has reached the end of the California continent, for to pass beyond he must embark." It was a prophetic remark, for a number of years passed before the bay waters to the north were crossed to establish a mission. But if Father Francis had reached "the end of the Cal-

ifornia continent," it seemed only fitting that the northernmost mission be named in his honor. And so in October 1776, the Mission of St. Francis de Asis was founded near San Francisco Bay.

The site, however, was not chosen by Father Serra, but by the Spanish captain Juan Bautista de Anza early in 1776, on the feast of Our Lady of Sorrows. For this reason "Mission Dolores" (Sorrows) is its most common title.

Facing page: Fray Junipero Serra, the founder of the California missions, is also known as the Apostle of California. Arriving in the New World in 1750 at age 37, this Franciscan friar was a missionary for 18 years among the Indians of Mexico. He did not begin his work with the California Indians until 1769 at age 56. Over the next 15 years, until his death in 1784, he developed Spain's plan for establishing a system of missions in California, and founded nine missions himself. He was tireless, fearless, sometimes quarrelsome, extremely devout, unselfish, and single-minded. He was an excellent administrator and many believe also a saint. Courtesy, Bancroft Library

Above: In 1816 a Russian expeditionary party entered San Francisco Bay on the vessel Rurik. Ludovic Choris, the illustrator on board, drew this scene of Indians dancing before the Mission St. Francis de Asis (Mission Dolores). Though the mission Indians were required to live a regimented life of work and worship, the Franciscans permitted them to continue their native dances within the mission walls. Courtesy, Bancroft Library

Mission Dolores was slow in developing, for the supply line to the north was remote and the laborers few. Not until 1782 were the first trees hewn for construction of the chapel, and it was not completed until 1791. From the beginning, the Mission received Indians from other parts of the bay, including Marin County and the Santa Clara valley. By 1810, almost 4,000 baptisms had been recorded at St. Francis' own mission.

The cost for these successes, however, had been high. Almost from the beginning, the Indians had been sickly, and disease swept through Mission Dolores on many occasions. In 1810, the number of deaths actually exceeded the number of births. The mortality rate among the San Francisco Indians was the highest of any of the missions, and a solution had to be found to prevent further decline among the Indian population.

If the Franciscan friars were disturbed by the condition of their northernmost mission, the Spanish authorities were concerned about more secular and political matters in the form of the menacing presence of Russian fur traders. By the time San Francisco Bay was discovered, the Russians had established precarious settlements off the Alaskan coast in pursuit of the pelts of the sea otter, and they had heard of the fabled California where the sea otter was in great abundance.

At the beginning of the nineteenth century, the bay of San Francisco and the lands surrounding it were in the primitive state they had been in for thousands of years. On the land, antelope and elk grazed on the hillsides of today's Marin County. The redwood forests of Mount Tamalpais were home to the powerful grizzly bear, which the Miwoks both feared and honored. Within the Indian settlements themselves, the coyote was a constant scavenger, a lurking thief.

The waters of the bay were almost more profligate than the land. Besides the ducks and geese of the tule marshes, fish were plentiful, with salmon spawning up the creeks on Marin's eastern coast. Whales surfacing near today's Alcatraz Island were a common sight, spouting streams of water as they moved through San Pablo Bay into the strait of Carquinez. The surface of the water was broken by vast herds of sea otter, especially near the rocky shoreline where mussels and abalone were abundant. The otters were so numerous they colored the water black, and canoes could pass over their silken, furry bodies, allowing the harpoon an easy entry. Much like the buffalo herds on the great

plains to the east, the supply of sea otters seemed endless.

In the spring of 1806, an event occurred that would have great significance for the founding of the Mission San Rafael and the development of the Marin peninsula. Nicholai Petrovich Rezanov, on a mission from the Russian Czar, entered San Francisco Bay on the *Juno*, which he had procured from Yankee traders who had entered into agreements with the Russians in Alaska as early as 1800. Rezanov had sailed from the north where he had visited half-starved Russians in settlements near present-day Sitka. He was seeking supplies for the Russians to the north, and at the same time was scouting for a more plentiful supply of sea otters and estimating the military strength of the Spanish in California.

The Russian visit became the occasion for one of California's first love stories when Rezanov sought and won the favor of Concepcion Arguello, the seventeen-year-old daughter of Jose David Arguello, the Spanish commander. When Rezanov sailed away on the *Juno*, he had not only his supplies, but also Arguello's blessing on his courtship. Rezanov planned to return and claim his bride, but died on his way back

to Russia. Concepcion waited 35 years for news of her lover's death, then entered the religious life, becoming a nun in Benecia.

Only a few years later, in 1809, the Spanish learned that the Russians had built a settlement at Bodega, near Point Reyes. In 1812, they learned that a fort, Fort Ross, had been built farther up the coast. Like the Franciscans, the Russians also built chapels with crosses and church bells. (It is interesting to note that the Catholic Church in Rome and the Russian Orthodox Church in Constantinople did, after a course of many centuries, move in opposite directions around the globe to end up only a few miles apart in northern California.) In addition to representing a territorial threat, the Russians also represented a religious interest, which could, and did, compete for the allegiance of the California Indians.

It is little wonder that both military and missionary ambitions turned the eyes of the Spaniards north to the Marin hills. Then, as now, the damp, cold, and inclement weather of the San Francisco peninsula magically vanished as one passed north, and the hills were bathed in sunshine. If the warmer climate of Marin might improve the ailing Indians at Mission Dolores, a mission settlement there would also serve as a warning to the encroaching Russians.

It was the Spanish governor, Pablo de Sola, who first suggested, as an experiment, that some San Francisco Indians live on the northern shore. When their health improved, the Spanish decided to establish an *asistencia,* a hospital mission. The Franciscans were eager for the move, for it would not only improve the health of the Indians but enable them to convert others in this uncivilized land. Father Gil y Taboado, who had some medical experience and who volunteered to

live among the Indians, was chosen to be the first director. In a letter to Governor Sola, the priest said, "I am ready to sacrifice myself in service of these poor Indians even to the shedding of my blood if necessary."

It was an auspicious day, on December 13, 1817, when Father Gil y Taboado, Father Prefect Vicente Francisco de Sarria, Father Ramon Abella of Mission Dolores, and Father Narciso Duran of San Jose, embarked for the Marin shores with a military escort under Jose Herrara. The site of the new mission was to be in the sunny valley where the city of San Rafael now lies, in a place the Indians called Nanaguani. It would be the twentieth mission in California. The name of the new mission was to be San Rafael, in honor of the healing messenger of God, the Archangel Rafael. The name was well chosen, for the Mission San Rafael would have one of the lowest death rates of any of the California missions.

Facing page: The redwood chapel of the Russian settlement of Fort Ross was constructed in the early 1820s. Located about thirty miles north of Bodega Bay on the Sonoma coast, it marks the deepest penetration of permanent Russian settlement into California. In the front is the bell tower and in the rear the cupola over the altar within. This 1901 photograph shows the work of restoration by then-owner George W. Call. A few years later, in 1906, the San Francisco Earthquake struck, and the chapel was badly damaged, but since has been fully restored. Courtesy, Bancroft Library

Above: Bernard du Hautcilly sketched the settlement at Fort Ross at the height of occupation in 1828. Fort Ross has the distinction of being the only Russian settlement within the continental United States, besides the Alaskan settlement at Sitka, New Archangel, established in 1799. Fort Ross was sold by the Russians to John Sutter in 1841 because the supply of sea otters had declined. Courtesy, Bancroft Library

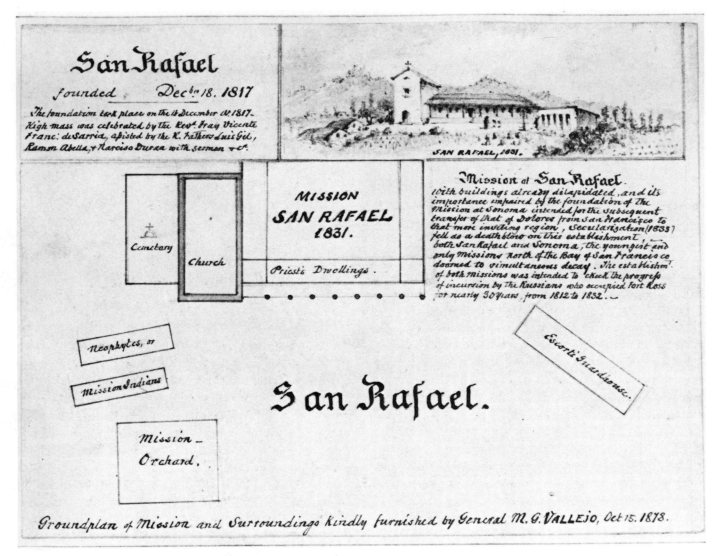

These Edward Vischer drawings show the ground plan and surroundings of the Mission San Rafael Arcangel as it appeared in 1831. The priests' dwellings were inside the church while the Spanish soldiers and the Indian neophytes had their ranchitos close to the mission building. Courtesy, Bancroft Library

Father Sarria decided that the founding celebration would include the full rites for a mission, not only because they had not been performed for over ten years, but because the Indians would be mightily impressed by the liturgy, the chants, and the incense. If, later, he wished to elevate the *asistencia,* a simple order would enable it to become a full-fledged mission (as indeed happened in 1823).

By the time Father Sarria and his company arrived on the Marin shore, it was nearly dark, and the formal dedication would have to await a new day. That evening, Father Sarria planted the cross, had vespers, and the friars sang the *Te Deum.* On the following morning, Mass was celebrated, and four baptisms were performed. About a year later, the then-president of the missions, Father Mariano Payeras, passed through the new mission and noted simply, "In the lee of Mount Tamalpais and beneath a line of rolling, tawny hills, crowned here and there with live oaks, the Mission was founded on December 14, 1817."

Father Gil y Taboado proved to be an able administrator, who also spoke the Miwok tongue. Born in Santa Fe in today's New Mexico, he was unusual among the Franciscans, for most were born in Spain. Father Sarria assigned him 230 ailing Indians, transferred from Mission Dolores, and by the end of the first year 386 newly baptized, or neophyte, Indians were resident at the new mission.

By the end of 1818, a tile-roofed adobe structure had been built, 87 feet long, 42 feet wide, and 18 feet high. It contained a chapel and a room for Father Gil, apartments for the military guards, and a guest room—all that was necessary in those spartan times, for the Indians lived outside in their village, or what the Spanish called their *ranchitos,* or "little ranches." The mission at San Rafael had no bell tower, but rather a sturdy frame outside the chapel from which hung the bells summoning the neophytes to work or prayer. Beyond the building and the church bells were laid out the agricultural fields, the orchards, vineyards, and vegetable gardens, all in close proximity to indicate that work and prayer were one.

In addition to the physical improvements, Father Gil recorded the first marriage performed at San Rafael, between Jose Maria, an Indian widower from the ranchito Liluangelia, and his Indian wife, Maria Josefa, from the ranchito Saconchini. He also recorded the first death at San Rafael, a 26-year-old Miwok man whose baptismal name was simply "Indian Rafael."

In 1819 Father Gil y Taboada suffered a heart attack and was replaced by Father Juan Amoros, a man who was destined to leave the most lasting impression upon the new Mission San Rafael. Every account of Father Amoros shows him to be as wise and good as he was intelligent. Though known widely for his sanctity, he also had human qualities that endeared him to many. Even those who were sometimes hostile to the missions—men like historian Hubert H. Bancroft and the Mexican general Mariano Vallejo—agree on his virtue and ability. It was under Father Amoros that the San Rafael Mission flourished.

The new mission had begun as a medical appendage to Mission Dolores to handle the overflow of sick Indians, but it soon established itself as an independent mission of considerable productivity. The fields were laid out with wheat, barley, corn, beans, and peas, and the bushel count increased steadily to over 4,000 per year in the early years. As late as 1841, an overland immigrant named John Bidwell—later an influential agriculturalist and politician—maintained that the grapes of San Rafael were the best of any mission.

Cattle, which had numbered only in the hundreds in the early years, had reached over 2,000 by 1830.

There were 4,000 sheep along with 450 horses. To accommodate those large numbers, the mission extended its boundaries to include most of what we know today as Marin County, with the exception of a buffer zone at Sausalito and at Point Reyes as a protection against the Russians. Mission San Rafael was Marin's only Spanish land grant, and its cattle and sheep grazed as far north as today's Novato.

At the mission itself, sheds and workshops for tanning leather, making harnesses, and for the construction and repair of tools were set up. Unlike the Russian settlement up the coast, no windmill or forge was ever built, but the various shops served both for production and for instruction of the Indians in the agricultural arts. Also at this time the mission's original structure became L-shaped through several new additions. A separate church was built and walls were constructed around the cemetery and orchard.

Success in the field and pasture was matched by success in the spiritual realm, and by 1828 over a thousand neophytes were living among the Franciscan friars and Spanish soldiers. To accommodate the increase in numbers, four two-story buildings were erected, with living quarters above and storage and work areas below. A separate house for single women was set aside, a common practice in the California missions.

The treatment of the San Rafael Indians was no better or worse than at any of the other missions. They lived by the sound of the church bells summoning them to prayer and to work. If they escaped, they were punished, sometimes by flogging or incarceration in wooden stocks. However we view today the kind of punishment that was common to Europeans of the time, it is nonetheless clear that the aim of the missions was not the destruction of the Indians, but their salvation. In retrospect, it was not the severity of the physical punishment that decimated the mission Indians, but rather the diseases of the Europeans, and something subtler than illness. For a people accustomed to living by the seasons, the migration of birds and the habits of animals, the church bells represented the daily work-a-day world for which they had little understanding and for which they were unprepared. Their dislocation from the land, divorced from life among the plants and animals, and their social disintegration, coupled with illnesses they could not fail to contract, are the true causes of the end of the ways of the Miwok.

The year 1823 was an eventful one for Mission San Rafael, for in that year it became fully independent from Mission Dolores, fulfilling the wise decision of Father Prefect Sarria to give it the full liturgical rites when founded in 1817. Not only had the mission become a productive settlement, but Father Amoros had even established a small chapel to the north in the Santa Rosa Valley where the most hostile of the Indians lived. With Franciscan fervor, he was constantly seeking new converts among the northern Indians, while fully aware that his religious forays were also building a bulwark against the Russian encroachment.

Indeed, the zeal to expand the kingdom of God on earth was widely shared among the Franciscans, especially in the person of Father Jose Altimira, a young priest stationed at Mission Dolores. Convinced that neither Mission Dolores nor San Rafael was adequate for the needs, he proposed they be abandoned and a new mission established, a mission he called the "new San Francisco." Without consulting his superiors, he secured the permission of California's acting governor, Luis Arguello, and reconnoitered the area north and east above San Pablo Bay, what we now know as the town of Sonoma.

News of Father Altimira's audacious plan reached the ears of Father Amoros, who informed Father Sarria, at that time father president of the missions. Sarria, the very celebrant of the founding Mass for San Rafael, was not about to see his northern missions dismantled. He proposed a compromise: let plans for the newest mission, to be called San Francisco Solano, continue, but maintain the other two missions as well, with the neophytes themselves deciding at which one to reside. Governor Arguello agreed, and in this transaction 92 neophytes were reassigned to San Francisco Solano. In this way the twenty-first, and last, California mission was established at Sonoma.

Eighteen twenty-three was the year that the Mission received both its independence and a threat to its existence, and the next year, 1824, saw a serious Indian uprising. It occurred late in the evening when Corporal Rafael Garcia and three soldiers were asleep.

The Indians were in force and bent upon massacre. The story, told by former California Governor Juan B. Alvarado, gives credit to Garcia for taking his own wife and children, along with Father Amoros, to the water's edge where they were placed on a tule reed boat to reach safety on the opposite shore. The valiant Garcia held off the Indians until Ignacio Martinez, the commander of the Presidio, arrived with soldiers to rout the Indians.

During that year, hostilities against Mission San Rafael were led by two Indians who have left their names on our history. According to reports, Chief Marin and Quentin were pursued by Commander Martinez of the mission's guard and took refuge on what we now know as the Marin Islands just off San Rafael. And while Marin escaped, Quentin was captured and imprisoned. His name endures on San Quentin Point and, appropriately, the state prison located upon it. Chief Marin later became a skilled boatman, called in Spanish "el marinero," from whence his name, and ultimately the name of the county, probably derived.

There is little question that Mission San Rafael experienced both tranquil and violent times, and no particular account or record can give the whole picture. Yet one of the best descriptions comes from an unlikely source, from the diary of the famous Russian explorer, Otto von Kotzebue, a man who three times circumnavigated the globe and was a captain in the Imperial Navy. In 1824, the very time of the Indian uprising and a time also of great productivity at the mission, von Kotzebue traveled north on horseback toward Fort Ross. The mission was along the route, and like other travelers he paused to gaze upon the church and

the garrison. Von Kotzebue was not the first or last such traveler between the fort and church of the Roman Catholics and the fort and church of the Russian Orthodox, for there was commerce between them. Yet his particular description catches both the beauty and peril of the early years of the founding of Mission San Rafael:

The locality of this mission . . . is still better chosen than that of the celebrated Santa Clara. A mountain shelters it from the injurious northwind; but the same mountain serves also as a hiding-place and bulwark for the *Indianos bravos* . . . [Next day] we mounted our horses and the fine, light, and fertile soil we rode upon was thickly covered with rich herbage, and the luxuriant trees stood in groups as picturesque as if they had been disposed by the hand of taste.

The founding of the mission and its survival against the forces of nature and of hostile Indians is one part of the story of San Rafael. The demise of the mission, and its passage from Spanish rule, first to Mexico and second to the United States, is quite another.

Facing page: When Russian illustrator Ludovic Choris drew these five Indians at the Mission St. Francis de Asis, their faces revealed the boredom and indifference that many travelers noted among mission Indians. The combination of widespread sickness, many deaths, and the loss of their way of life produced a malaise reflected in their demeanor. Courtesy, Bancroft Library

Above: The method of warfare between Spanish soldiers and California Indians is depicted in this 1971 drawing by Spanish artist Jose Cardero. It is the first known illustration of the Spanish soldier in action in California. An Indian on foot was no match for a Spaniard on horseback. Courtesy, Bancroft Library

UNDER TWO FLAGS

The extension of the Franciscan missions into Alta California had come at a time of great significance for liberty-loving peoples in both the Old and the New worlds. The English colonies on the eastern seaboard declared their independence the very year Mission Dolores was founded, and by the time the Mission San Rafael was established, the effects of the French Revolution of 1789 were being felt throughout the colonies of New Spain. Men such as Simon Bolivar were leading military campaigns throughout present-day Venezuela and Colombia against the Spanish crown, inspiring the colonists in Mexico to overthrow the Spanish monarchy in 1821. The Mexican flag now flew over California.

These events were felt throughout the missions and reached Mission San Rafael in the form of a Mexican Constitution, which the Franciscans regarded as anti-clerical. Like many others, Father Juan Amoros was asked to swear allegiance to the new Constitution, but unlike others, he would not swear the oath. Rather, he promised the Mexican authorities that he would obey the civil authority so long as it did not require him to violate his conscience. Under other circumstances, the Mexicans might have relieved him, but there was no one to replace Juan Amoros.

The mission system, including San Rafael, had grown large and prosperous, due in large part to men like Father Amoros. It is estimated that, from the founding of the first mission (San Diego) in 1769 to the time of Mexican independence, the twenty-one missions had 10,000 acres under cultivation and owned 60,000 horses, 400,000 cattle, and 300,000 hogs, sheep, and goats. Far more than merely churches

Above: John Charles Fremont had a long and colorful career after his surveying expeditions in the West and his role in supporting the Bear Flag Republic. For a short period he served as governor of California, until court-martialed by General Stephen Kearney, tried, and found guilty of mutiny. In 1856 he was nominated for president by the new Republican Party but was defeated by James Buchanan. In 1878 he was appointed governor of the Arizona Territory. This circa 1850 engraving shows him in his uniform as a major general in the U.S. Army. Courtesy, Bancroft Library

Facing page; General Mariano Guadalupe Vallejo was the undisputed ruler of California's northern frontier under Mexican rule. He was a student of military affairs and ancient history and he wrote a history of California. He was unexcelled as a leader of men and an excellent tactician on the battlefield. Though a citizen of Mexico, Vallejo greatly admired the Americans and sympathized with them during the Mexican-American War. This youthful portrait depicts him in the 1830s. Courtesy, Bancroft Library

and a collection of Indian converts, the missions were flourishing economic and social settlements, which, in 1821, were more powerful than the new Mexican government.

Before long, the power balance was redressed. In 1833 the Mexican Congress passed the Secularization Bill, whereby, in the following year, the missions were to be converted to *pueblos,* or towns. Because the Revolution itself had been inspired in part by the condition of the oppressed Indians in New Spain and throughout the Caribbean, secularization decreed that one half of the mission lands, livestock, and property be distributed to the neophytes, with the remainder placed under the care of an administrator appointed by the governor.

Just a year earlier, in 1832, Father Juan Amoros had died, and the task of secularizing the missions was left to Mexican Franciscans. Those who followed Father Amoros were not as capable as he, and historical accounts are not kind to his successors, who were caught up in the problems of this transition period between sacred and secular authorities, and who lacked the qualities of mind and character to overcome them.

With the Secularization Bill, one era in Marin's history ended and another began. The Franciscans and the Spaniards were replaced by the Mexican *Californios* (those born in California of Spanish parents) and by the European settlers who were allied with them. With secularization, the vast Mission San Rafael was divided into over twenty Mexican land grants between 1834 and 1846. One such grant was given in 1835 to the neophytes, the Indians, of Mission San Rafael,

who chose a large inland territory known as Nicasio. Even though it was clearly deeded to them by the Mexican governor, they were never able to secure clear title to the 80,000-acre land grant and eventually lost it in a suspicious transaction. A more successful Indian acquisition is represented by Camilo Ynitia, who was given the old Miwok territory of Olompali in 1843. Ynitia was an able man who learned Spanish, adopted European ways, and became a close friend of Vallejo. He apparently sold the disputed rights to Olompali for $5,000, and at his death in 1856 left a substantial legacy to his family.

The foremost *Californio* in the northern region was without doubt Mariano Guadalupe Vallejo. His lineage was impressive, tracing back to a victorious Captain Vallejo with the conquering Cortes in Mexico, and even earlier to Admiral Vallejo, who had com-

---

Above: This painting shows General Vallejo reviewing his troops in 1836 before the Mission St. Francis de Solano in Sonoma. Mission San Rafael was also within Vallejo's military jurisdiction and he took cattle and property from it to support the Mission at Sonoma. From this farthest outpost, Vallejo led expeditions against the Indians in today's Napa Valley and maintained the peace north and east for a hundred miles. Courtesy, Bancroft Library

Facing page: At roundup time, the Californios singled out young livestock and marked their hindquarters with a red-hot branding iron. Even though each iron was properly registered with the authorities there was sometimes confusion over cattle ownership, which led to rustling and occasional violence between ranchers. Painting by Edward Vischer. Courtesy, Bancroft Library

manded the ship carrying Columbus back to Spain in irons. The Admiral's brother, Don Pedro Vallejo, was a Viceroy of New Spain. The father of Mariano Vallejo, Don Ignacio, had been a member of the military guard protecting Father Junipero Serra early in his career.

Born in 1808, Mariano Vallejo was raised at the presidio in Monterey and rose quickly in the military ranks. By 1835, he had been named commander of the northern frontier, with headquarters in Sonoma. Though a child of the Church, he was hostile to the missions, thinking that the Franciscans badly misunderstood military matters. His teachers were rather the Roman Emperors, and he looked favorably upon the Caesars in following the policy of "divide and conquer." In his own history of California, Vallejo argues that the only way the few Europeans were able to withstand the more numerous Indians was by his policy of pitting one Indian tribe against another.

As remarkable as Vallejo was, neither he nor the Mexican authorities could achieve their objective of consolidating Mexican political power without the help of foreign settlers who, at that time, numbered less than a dozen on the Marin peninsula.

One of the earliest settlers was John Reed, who, born in Dublin in 1805, had arrived in San Francisco by way of Acapulco in 1826. He became friendly with the commander of the Presidio, Jose Antonio Sanchez, and also with Father Juan Amoros. He then traveled north of the Mission, to present day Cotati, and began farming. When hostile Indians captured his cattle and drove him off, Reed returned to the Mission, finally settling in Sausalito. In the same year of the Secularization Bill (1833), Reed followed the path of sure success in dealing with the new Mexican government: he became a Mexican citizen. A few months later, Reed received the first Mexican land grant north of San Francisco Bay, "Corte Madera del Presidio," which literally means "the cut wood of the Presidio," so named because Reed provided the Mexican military with wood. His land grant included Belvedere and the entire Tiburon peninsula opposite Richardson's Bay—a total of 7,845 acres.

John Reed was the kind of European the Mexican authorities liked and trusted. They displayed that trust by choosing him as the *majordomo* of the San Rafael mission in 1836, charging him with the disbursal of the mission lands. Reed remained in the post only one year, turning it over to the man who was to be the real custodian of the last days of the Mission San Rafael.

That man was Timothy Murphy, also an Irishman, and known affectionately as "Don Timoteo." In 1837 he was appointed administrator of the mission, as well as the agent for some 1,400 Indians, and was named *alcalde* of San Rafael. Murphy was a character almost larger than life. Well over six-feet tall and weighing 300 pounds, Don Timoteo appeared like a giant to the Indians, who looked up to him as a father. He spoke their language with an Irish brogue and encouraged them to use the skills they had learned at the Mission. His advice was good because the Indians, freed from the regimen of mission life, had little but agricultural skills to sustain them in the new society. Each of the ranchos represented by the land grants required workers. And there is no doubt it was the Indians trained at Mission San Rafael who became the first laborers in Marin County under the Mexican *Californios*.

Timothy Murphy is not only remembered for his treatment of the Indians but for his friendship with Mariano Vallejo, the real power in northern California. He almost married into the family, courting Vallejo's sister, Donna Rosalio, but she declined his suit and he died a bachelor. It was Vallejo who ordered Murphy to move the cattle and grapes from the Mis-

sion to his own rancho in Sonoma and who sent Don Timoteo to England to purchase purebred sheep, cattle, and swine to develop his own herds.

Murphy himself, in 1844, received from the Mexicans a 22,000-acre land grant at San Rafael, called "Santa Margarita, Las Gallinas and San Pedro." It included the northeastern part of San Rafael proper, stretching north to present-day Northgate, Terra Linda, Marinwood, and Lucas Valley, as well as east to San Pedro Point, today's McNear's Beach, and China Camp. A year later, in 1845, Murphy built a two-story adobe house that served as the center of town and from which he greeted visitors to the mission for Sunday Mass after a night of feasting and revelry.

One such night was October 24, 1841, celebrated in honor of the feast of St. Rafael Arcangel and called "San Rafael Day." *Rancheros,* soldiers, and visitors from miles around were invited to come, including members of the U.S. exploring expedition under Commander Charles Wilkes, whose ship was at anchor in Sausalito harbor. The chief feature was to be a fight between a bull and a grizzly bear, a fight in which the bear usually won. On this day, no grizzly could be found, yet the festivities went on, and the evening party more than made up for the disappointment. It was the first recorded "San Rafael Day."

Those were "the days of the dons," when the power of Spain had been broken and the new secular power, Mexico, was not yet strong enough to rule independently. Men like Reed and Murphy—along with Captain William Richardson who married a Mexican woman and received a 19,000-acre land grant in Sausalito, and who was named Port Captain of Yerba Buena (San Francisco) in 1837—were the necessary instruments of Mexican rule. It was a time in which the phrase "the fat of the land" was heard, a time when there was a servant class of Indians, bountiful lands and wild game, and even wine pressed from mission grapes to adorn groaning tables. Evening parties characteristically continued until dawn, and the fandangoes of the Spanish were danced by all. With an increasing number of Yankee ships bringing silk dresses from New England and elegant household goods, the women of the grantees proved more than hospitable. The parties at the homes of Reed and Murphy were renowned, and they brought high officials from the Presidio and a growing number of merchants, traders, and visitors from Yerba Buena (San Francisco) across the bay. The gaiety and music and mixed company of those long and pleasurable evenings were in marked contrast to the austere religious celebrations of the mission days, and already San Rafael was becoming known as a center of social life.

If the relations between the *Californios* and the Europeans were cordial in Marin County during the days of Mexican rule, they were quite otherwise between

the Mexicans and the Yankees in other parts of California. By this time, the sea route from America's eastern ports such as Boston and New York, around the Horn of South America to San Francisco, was well established. In 1847, the name "Yerba Buena" was dropped in favor of "San Francisco," and the active

and busy port brought merchants and traders and businessmen from eastern cities.

The land routes also had been opened up, first by the Lewis and Clark expedition of 1804-1806 into Oregon, and later by Jedediah Smith, who, in 1826, became the first white man to reach California overland. Hunters and trappers followed his trail as they pursued the rich pelts of the beaver. In the 1840s when the supply of beaver all but vanished, they still pushed westward, entering the valley of the San Joaquin and eventually the port of San Francisco.

As the Yankee immigrants saw more of the land, they were seized by the conviction that California had the potential of developing a more productive economy. The *Californios* seemed indolent and lacking in the discipline and industry required to make the land something more than a mere cattle range. Historian Allen R. Nevins has written:

The tensions between the races was already painful. Not merely did the Americans regard the natives as lazy, child-

---

Facing page: As this 1830s illustration shows, life on the frontier of northern California was often dull, and the ranchers sometimes found entertainment in pitting a bull against a grizzly bear. Though not natural enemies, the animals were enclosed in a small pen, making a bloody encounter inevitable. Since both animals were ultimately to be destroyed, the ranchers thought it no loss to have them battle to the death. The grizzly bear usually won. Courtesy, Society of California Pioneers

Above, right: Mountain men were a tough breed of isolated hunters who trapped beavers and killed bears for their furs. As the animals declined in number, the trappers moved westward into California and settled there. They were fiercely independent men who pushed America's frontiers ever westward in accordance with the idea of Manifest Destiny. They were often hostile to the Californios and joined with American settlers against the Mexicans. Drawing by Frederic Remington. Courtesy, Bancroft Library

like, untruthful and cowardly. The Californians, for their part, tended to look upon the immigrants as rough, over-bearing and grasping—as brutal fellows whose one aim was gain. In general, mutual understanding was impossible. Protestant against Catholic, Anglo-Saxons against Latins, strenuous pioneers against idlers—they were sundered by instinctive antipathies.

The growing number of Yankee immigrants to California gave them the confidence to believe that some day the land would be theirs. The American belief in "Manifest Destiny" seemed to require a march westward to the very shores of the Pacific. Rumor of war with Mexico had been rampant in the early 1840s following an edict of Governor Juan Bautista Alvarado that all Yankees and Englishmen were to be arrested—and some were. Fifty settlers were actually sent to Mexico in chains.

Into this cauldron of hostile feelings rode John C. Frémont, the man who would be responsible for carrying into Marin County the Yankee ambition to conquer Mexico, and who would initiate several brutal murders that radically changed the amicable relations with the Mexicans.

Frémont was an officer in the Topographical Corps of the U.S. Army, and he led several successful surveying expeditions along the Oregon Trail with the legendary scout, Kit Carson. Early in May 1846, after receiving a hurried message from his superiors in Washington carried by a young lieutenant named Archibald Gillespie, Frémont turned back from his surveying tasks in Oregon and entered California. His coming attracted a motley group of hunters, trappers, and mountain men eager to do battle with the Mexicans.

All the elements for a small war in northern California were present when the fuse was lit by a group of Yankee settlers who intercepted a force led by Mexican Lieutenant Francisco Arce, who was taking 170 horses, recently collected at Mission San Rafael, to army headquarters in Santa Clara. After seizing the horses, the settlers moved north toward the Sonoma mission.

It was there on June 14, 1846, with the support of Frémont, that about thirty Yankees descended upon the Mexican fort at Sonoma and captured Mariano Vallejo and his brother Salvador. It is ironic that Vallejo, who actually supported the American claim to California, should have been the pawn in this early

outbreak of the Mexican-American war. With typical hospitality, Vallejo offered his captors liquor from his own cabinet.

This aggressive act was the Bear Flag Revolt, and the Yankees, eager to justify their actions, hastily created a flag with a star in the corner and a grizzly bear in the center. Four days later, on June 18, William B. Ide solemnly declared the establishment of the "Bear Flag Republic." The justification to create a new "republic" and so disguise the real desire of the Yankees to take over California was not, in retrospect, necessary; one month earlier, on May 12, 1846, the United States had indeed declared war on Mexico, but the news had not reached distant California.

With Sonoma secure, two members of the Bear Flag party, William Fowler and Thomas Cowie, traveled to nearby Santa Rosa to procure gunpowder. On

Facing page: This 1860s photograph of General Mariano Vallejo with several of his daughters and granddaughters shows him in late middle age after California's admission to the Union in 1850. Vallejo was military commander of Alta California, and his influence was felt for many decades. His home, "Lachryma Montis" (The Tears of the Mountain), with its gardens and orchards, lay just outside Sonoma and is now a California historical landmark. Courtesy, Bancroft Library

Above: The Bear Flag was raised over the Mexican fort of Sonoma on June 14, 1846. Pictured above is the Bear Flag owned by Patrick McChristian, a member of the Bear Flaggers, as they were called, who captured General Vallejo and several others. As the first act of defiance against the Mexican government, the Bear Flaggers were reluctant to fly the Stars and Stripes, so in its place they flew the Bear Flag. In memory of the short-lived Bear Flag Republic, California included a bear on its state flag. Courtesy, Society of California Pioneers

the way they were captured by a small band of *Californios* headed by a former alcalde of Yerba Buena, Juan Padilla, who had just received the last of the land grants constituting the Mission San Rafael, the Bolsa de Tomales. Historians disagree on who was responsible for the deaths of Fowler and Cowie, though the blame at the time was placed squarely on Padilla or one of his men. Regardless, the bodies were discovered and they had been hacked and cut horribly by a dagger. Now thoroughly alarmed that the hunters would become the hunted, Padilla and his men rode to the second largest settlement of the San Rafael mission, Olompali, where they encountered about fifty Mexican soldiers under the command of Lieutenant de la

Torre, a force that was hastily organized after the news of the Bear Flag Revolt.

When news of the aroused Mexicans reached Sonoma, the Bear Flag party responded by alerting Lieutenant Frémont and organizing a force led by one of the Bear Flaggers, Lieutenant William Ford, to attack de la Torre. The two forces met on June 24 at Olompali, and after a brief skirmish, in which one Mexican was killed and two wounded, Ford and his men retreated to Sonoma. The war in the area of the San

Rafael mission had now accounted for three lives but the killings were not yet over. Frémont, along with Kit Carson and a group of 160 men, including savage Delaware Indians carrying spiked maces, now moved swiftly toward San Rafael where they supposed the outnumbered forces of de la Torre would be. Frémont and his men stormed the mission, only to discover that the fleet-footed Mexicans had already passed by, heading for Sausalito.

De la Torre and Juan Padilla now turned to one of the Europeans who had always been on excellent terms with the Mexicans, Captain William Richardson of Sausalito. Fortunately, a record exists of that encounter, in the words of his son, Stephen Richardson. He wrote:

The half-armed troops of De la Torre were no match for the disciplined troops under Frémont . . . It was a demoralized mob of fugitives that arrived in Sausalito at midnight and knocked on the Richardson family residence . . . They seemed to think that Frémont and his men were only a few jumps behind them. They described the Delaware Indians as each equal to a dozen devils rolled into one.

Young Richardson then described the pleas of the Mexicans for assistance and noted that all the settled foreigners in the region sympathized with the *Californios* against Frémont. He said:

Why would they not have been sympathetic? They had come here, strangers, nearly all penniless, had received the hand of friendship, and been given lands and wealth, and had intermarried with the people. Why should they not have felt grateful and more than well disposed toward a generous, open-handed people?

The response of Captain Richardson to the Mexicans was "There is my schooner at the wharf. I do not see how I can stop you from taking it. I am over-powered by numbers, and resistance would be idle on my part."

The next morning, Frémont arrived in high dudgeon, bitterly disappointed that he had lost his prey. Stephen Richardson recalled him: "He had a fine, soldierly bearing—the make-up commands obedience—but oh, what an eye! It was like the eye of some great predacious creature—cold, restless, unforgiving."

Frustrated in his pursuit of de la Torre, Frémont returned to San Rafael, and the stage was set for the murder of three innocent *Californios*. According to Stephen Richardson's account, Jose Berryessa (an old

man whose son was the alcalde at Sonoma) had come to the mission with his two nephews, Francisco and Ramon de Haro, to inquire about the Sonoma situation. They planned to borrow mission horses and ride there. The three men tied up their boat at the landing spot on the San Rafael Creek, just a short walk from the mission where both Kit Carson and John Frémont were quartered. The next series of events are obscure, but the result was the killing of three unarmed men. And while Carson is usually charged with the crimes, the scholar Arthur Quinn concludes, "whether Carson or Frémont was directly responsible for the deaths, the act was in character for both men. Carson would simply have done it as a matter of course, for the fun of it; Frémont would have given it an epic justification."

The events at San Rafael were only a small part of the tapestry of war woven by much larger forces. When the Bear Flag Republic was being established, an army under General Zachary Taylor was already invading Mexico and storming Monterrey in the northern provinces. In the next year, 1847, General Winfield Scott entered Mexico City with his victorious army, and the Mexicans sued for peace. On February 2, 1848, the Treaty of Guadalupe Hidalgo was signed, giving all Mexican lands north of the Rio Grande to the United States. Manifest Destiny—a single nation from the Atlantic to the Pacific—had been achieved.

It is interesting to note that one week before, on January 24, 1848, James Wilson Marshall had discovered gold at Coloma, on the south fork of the American River, beginning the greatest Gold Rush in history. It is at least arguable that, on that date, the land and its minerals legally belonged to Mexico, and, however late, the Spanish search for El Dorado proved not to have been in vain.

Events were moving rapidly for California now, and the First Constitutional Convention was held on September 3, 1849. A number of familiar names were present as delegates, including Mariano Vallejo, John A. Sutter, on whose land gold was first discovered, and Dr. Robert Semple, one of the original Bear Flag party. It was Semple who was elected president of the Assembly, and when the new constitution was ratified later that year, one of the two U.S. Senators was John C. Frémont. Early in 1850, Senator Frémont read a long speech to the U.S. Congress, arguing the admission of California to the Union. He was successful. On September 9, 1850, President Millard Fillmore signed the Admission Bill and California became the thirty-first state.

These national events were matched by decisions closer to home. California's first legislature met in February of 1850 and created twenty-seven counties, one of which was Marin County. And on April 15, 1851, the first governor of California, Peter H. Burnett, declared San Rafael the seat of justice in the county.

On those historic dates, the future of San Rafael was placed squarely into the hands of its own citizens. The Spaniards and the Russians were gone, and the Mexicans and the Indians remained only for a time. The future, and the fortunes, of the city and the county would be decided by the Yankees.

Facing page: Christopher "Kit" Carson was an Indian agent, frontiersman, and soldier, and was regarded as the most skillful and dependable guide of the early West. For 12 years, during his youth and early manhood, he was a mountain man; he married an Indian woman who bore him a daughter. He accompanied John Fremont from 1842 to 1846 during his surveying expeditions in the West. After the Mexican American War, Carson moved to Taos in the New Mexico Territory where he raised sheep, scouted for the Army, and fought against Apaches, Navajos, and Comanches. Near the end of his life (d. 1868) he was honored by being named a brevet brigadier general in the U.S. Army. Courtesy, Bancroft Library

Above, left: The Bear Flag Party, shown here in 1846 on the plaza of the Fort at Sonoma, was composed of 33 men headed by Ezekiel Merritt, Dr. Robert Semple, and William B. Ide. They called themselves "Los Osos" (The Bears) to assure anonymity. After capturing Mexican General Vallejo, his brother Salvador, and two others, they marched them to Sutter's Fort. The Bear Flag Republic lasted just 26 days until Captain John Fremont and his troops took over with the advent of the Mexican American War. Courtesy, Society of California Pioneers

CHAPTER 5

YANKEE SAN RAFAEL

The county seat of Marin County was a small settlement indeed in the 1850s. Its centerpiece was the old Mission, now crumbling away, which the San Francisco Archbishop, Joseph Alemany, described in 1855 as "an old miserable church and a few rooms in the same condition." Even so, the Short brothers, Jacob and John, had attached an addition to one end as a kind of dwelling. Timothy Murphy's two-story adobe house was the most impressive building, while nearby a general store had been erected in 1851 by John A. Davis and Daniel T. Taylor. Even earlier, in 1849, James Miller built a frame schoolhouse, the first in Yankee San Rafael. By 1858, a meat market with two rooms was constructed by Elisha DuBois and Ai Barney. One old-timer, A.C. McAllister, reminiscing at the turn of the century, declared, "All life and business was conducted on one little street of one little block."

Although the town was small, its citizens were farsighted. In 1850 Myers and McCullough completed a survey, and 48 blocks of 300 square feet each were laid out for future development. San Rafael Creek meandered as far up as First and D streets, where an old whale boat lay on its side.

In all of Marin County in 1850 there were only 321 people, about a fourth of whom were women. Perhaps half that number lived in or near San Rafael, many in the ranchos that dotted the hillsides. The residents had postal service with mail carried in on horseback from San Francisco through Benicia, Napa, and Sonoma, a circuitous route. The first postmaster, Moses Stoppard, was appointed in November 1851.

Already the county seat was being organized into four townships—Sausalito, Bolinas, Novato, and San Rafael. S.S. Baechtel was elected the first sheriff, and the first two lawyers admitted to practice were Walter

Facing page: The Pratt Building, at the corner of Fourth and B streets, served as a general merchandise store as well as saloon and liquor store. Note the sign advertising "Philadelphia Lager." The Pratt building was later purchased by one of San Rafael's leading merchants, Jacob Albert, who opened a dry goods store there near the turn of the century. Albert's store developed into a multi-million-dollar business with branches throughout Marin County and the East Bay. This photo was taken in the 1880s. Courtesy, Bancroft Library

Above: On the Fourth of July, 1858, Elisha DuBois and Ai Barney opened what was probably one of the first stores in San Rafael— a meat market. It was located on the east side of C Street between Third and Fourth streets. In this early 1860s photo, the partners and their friends pose in front of the market. DuBois came to San Rafael from Ohio in 1850, first as a cattleman, then as a butcher. Ai Barney became one of San Rafael's first citizens as judge and as newspaper publisher. Courtesy, Bancroft Library

Skidmore and J.H. Shelton. The first physicians were Dr. James A. Shorb and Dr. Alfred W. Taliaferro, the latter a Virginian and a well-beloved figure who healed first and sought payment, if any, later. Dr. Shorb served briefly as the first county judge, to be replaced by Ai Barney, who presided with distinction for seven years.

These activities were a clear sign of Yankee industry and of the system of county government that enabled smaller portions of the state to be developed under local control while the larger issues were handled by the legislature under state representatives. Marin's boundaries were actually fixed by its more powerful neighbors, San Francisco and Sonoma, when California's first legislature met in 1850. Marin County was sandwiched between them and denied access to a navigable port. San Francisco County was extended to Angel Island and Richardson's Bay, so that ocean-going vessels were under the legal jurisdiction of San Francisco. To the north, the deep channels of the Petaluma River were given to Sonoma County, a decision that not only eliminated a bay port for Marin but made certain that many goods from San Francisco would bypass it completely. It is for this reason that, in 1870, Petaluma was the sixth largest city in California and that passenger boats only stopped at San Rafael because it was on the way to the more important river town of Petaluma.

The business of San Rafael in Marin County was not shipping. Its real business was livestock—the cattle which roamed the sunny hillsides and valleys in vast herds of many thousands. Marin County was a principal source of beef both for the growing San Francisco and for the hungry prospectors up the Sacramento Delta and the foothills of the Sierra Nevada.

All the early residents comment on the dusty main street of San Rafael, today's Fourth Street, which was the thoroughfare for cattle driven off the hills to the west and north on their way to the San Francisco and Sacramento markets. Sometimes the *vaqueros* drove the cattle overland through Sonoma, Napa, and on to Marysville and Sacramento. To facilitate shipment to San Francisco, in the 1850s the firm of Clark and Moyland built a slaughterhouse on San Rafael Creek. It is reported that in some weeks as many as 100 head of cattle, with each steer worth twenty-five dollars and up, were killed and their carcasses transported by ship across the bay to San Francisco. One enterprising owner tried to swim his herd across the bay and lost

half of it. The names of some of the bay captains have come down to us as the first Yankee skippers connecting San Rafael with San Francisco: Captain Higgins in the sloop *Boston*, and Captain George Magee in "the finest sailing packet on the bay," the *Ida*.

Both San Rafael and Marin County grew slowly not only because of their inaccessibility across the churning tidal waters sweeping the Golden Gate, but also because of uncertainty over the possession of Mexican land grants. Cattle needed grazing land, and the question of land ownership bedeviled all the first families of Marin, the original grantees.

The full story of the Mexican land grants cannot be told here. The Mexicans had never accurately surveyed their territory, and the grants were bestowed without a clear description of the land. The grantee was given great discretion regarding its location, and there was no careful registry of the grants. The Americans, on the other hand, needed the land and found few signs of ownership. Some "squatters" were innocent and some were not, yet all hoped to claim the land they occupied either through the improvements made upon it or through the protection afforded by new federal laws. There were many disputes between the settlers and the Mexicans, and between the conflicting claims of various settlers almost to the time of the Civil War.

Figures tell the story. In 1850 there were 21 land grants in Marin County owned by former Mexican citizens. By 1866 all of the original grantees were gone.

There was no dispute, however, about the land grant on which San Rafael rested, the one known as "Santa Margarita, Las Gallinas and San Pedro." It belonged to Timothy Murphy, who died just two years after San Rafael became the county seat. Appropriately, the county office was then moved into Murphy's two-story adobe house, a decision he undoubtedly would have approved of. Prior to his death, Murphy had been provident in bringing his nephew John Lucas

---

Facing page: The first public library in San Rafael was located in the Franetta building, called "The San Rafael Bargain Store," from 1887 to 1903. Its second location was the old San Rafael High School, from 1903 to 1908. The public library was moved in 1909 to its third and present location, Fifth Avenue and Mission, when a new building was constructed with a grant from the Scottish philanthropist, Andrew Carnegie. Courtesy, San Rafael Public Library and Marin Independent Journal

and his brother Matthew over from Wexford County, Ireland, to assist him in managing his large estate.

His will revealed that John Lucas would receive the 2,340-acre "Santa Margarita Ranch," the area now known as Terra Linda and Lucas Valley, while the "Punta San Pedro" portion, today's McNear's Beach, Peacock Gap, and China Camp, would go to brother Matthew. The will was also generous to the Catholic Church. The present site of the San Rafael Mission and the Palace Hotel property in San Francisco was bequeathed, along with 680 acres north of San Rafael for "a seminary or institution of learning." Murphy's will required, however, that the "seminary or institution of learning" be functioning within two years or be forfeited. So it was that, in 1855, St. Vincent's Orphanage and School began operation, and it has continued to the present day.

The disposition of Murphy's land grant was also the process by which San Rafael has historically defined itself. Even at that time, the land north of the small settlement around the Mission was regarded as part of the town. When John Lucas was given the "Santa Margarita Rancho," he soon built a house for Maria Sweetman, his new bride from Ireland. The large, two-story home, in today's Terra Linda, was completed in 1867. In 1898, Manuel T. Freitas, a Portuguese dairyman, paid $80,000 for the house and ranch. Later it was torn down, providing the site for today's St. Isabella's Church and School, which, appropriately, is on the Manuel T. Freitas Parkway.

If one portion of San Rafael's original land grant suggests the boundaries of the city, another portion suggests the city's early commitment to learning. In 1845, Mary and James Miller arrived in San Rafael after having been in the famous "Murphy-Miller Party" under the leadership of Martin Murphy, the father of Mary. This expedition was the first to bring immigrants from Missouri to California without a single

loss of life. After reaching Sutter's Fort in December 1844, and following a six-week layover in Sacramento, the Miller family pushed on to San Rafael. They are believed to be the first settlers to reach San Rafael by the overland route.

A year after his arrival in San Rafael, James Miller purchased 680 acres from Timothy Murphy's "Las Gallinas Rancho," and with this transfer was completed one of Marin's first deeds. Using his ranch lands well, in 1849 Miller drove 150 head of cattle east to Marysville where he sold them at a fine profit to merchants providing beef to prospectors in the foothills of the Sierras. He soon became prosperous and later built a mansion for his large family of ten children. In 1880, it was described as "a square building, massive in appearance and commodiously apportioned into convenient apartments . . . the central figure of tastefully laid out grounds and well-wooded groves."

But the building for which James Miller is most remembered is the small frame building constructed in 1849 as the first school in San Rafael. He also financed the school that was located at the corner of today's Fourth and A streets. A priest from the Mission, Father Robetti, was the first instructor, though attor-

ney Walter Skidmore is also recorded as teaching in that same year. James Miller's dedication to education went beyond sectarian lines—in 1862 he donated land on which one of Marin's first public schools, the Dixie Public School, was later constructed.

The building of schoolhouses and homes by the first settlers suggests that the land grants were important for uses other than cattle. Upon the land grew the redwoods, which provided lumber for construction. And a man with the appropriate name of Isaac Shaver was the owner of one of the first sawmills in San Rafael.

Shaver was from New York, and, like many early settlers, had first tried mining after coming to California in 1858. After six years of middling luck near Placerville, he purchased the mill property of Dell and Holland in San Rafael and began operations. Not content with one mill, he established another in Nicasio Valley where 20,000 board feet of lumber was produced daily.

Sawing lumber is one thing; transporting it is quite another. It was easy enough to cart lumber by horse and wagon to the lots of San Rafael, but the need for houses in San Francisco required water transit. San

Rafael's port in these times was Ross Landing in present-day Kentfield. For years, flat-bottomed schooners were able to traverse the wide Corte Madera Slough with groceries and liquor from San Francisco and return with a cargo of firewood and lumber. Seeing the commercial possibilities, Isaac Shaver built his own wharf at Ross Landing in 1862 and ran a road across the hill to his sawmill in San Rafael. It was over this road—now known as Wolfe Grade to honor a druggist who lived on the San Rafael side—that Shaver transported lumber that went into many of the town's first and best homes.

Isaac Shaver's mill was only one of scores that soon became operational, mills that created small lumber boom towns, especially in west Marin near Bolinas, Olema, and Tomales. The forests around these towns were producing one million board feet of lumber a year, and with lumber selling at two dollars per board foot in San Francisco, small fortunes were being made. There was a wharf at Bolinas that enabled schooners to carry lumber directly to San Francisco through the Golden Gate.

Perhaps nothing better illustrates the instability and violence of this period than these lumber boom towns, where transient loggers came and went as the spirit moved them and as the pay was good or bad. An 1880 history of Marin County lists dozens of violent crimes with graphic descriptions of the killers, their motives, and their punishments. But not all murderers were captured; indeed, the largest number were not. Across the bay in San Francisco, hundreds of homicides occurred, but only a few of the killers were tried and convicted. In 1856 the situation became so desperate that a Vigilante Committee was formed, headed by William T. Coleman, a man who would later become a major figure in the development of San Rafael. It was Coleman and his committee who established a rough sort of justice in executing Charles Cora and James Casey for the murders of U.S. Marshal Richardson and newspaperman James King, after a "trial," which, though secret, followed commonly accepted judicial practices. The effects were very beneficial in restoring order.

History records no acts of violence around the mills of Isaac Shaver, but it does note how productive they

were and how necessary for the growth of San Rafael. Shaver's accomplishments were not only that he operated successful mills, but that he secured property for himself, built homes on divided lots, then rented them. By 1880 it was estimated that he owned seventy such structures, giving him the title of the largest landlord in town.

Another early sawmill owner was destined to have an even more profound effect on the county and its seat in San Rafael. His name was Ai Barney. Before coming to San Francisco in 1849, Barney had already enjoyed an impressive career. Born in Genoa, New York, he had mastered Latin and Greek as a young man, been a schoolmaster, then a justice of the peace in Frederick City, Maryland. Arriving in California seeking a good business venture, Ai Barney represented the Baltimore and Frederick Trading and Mining Company of Maryland, a group of thirty partners each of whom had contributed one thousand dollars to the venture.

Barney found his opportunity on the old Reed Rancho at "Corte Madera del Presidio"; he reestablished

---

Facing page: Isaac Shaver's planing mill was the first large industry in San Rafael. He located it in the early 1860s on the south side of Wolfe Grade with access to Ross Landing on the Corte Madera Creek. This drawing shows the mill, and horse-drawn wagons taking lumber toward Ross Landing for water transit to San Francisco, where the lumber was in great demand. Courtesy, Bancroft Library

Above, right: Though Ross Landing handled much of the water transport to San Francisco in the early years, San Rafael had its own landing. In this 1909 postcard view, a hay scow is loaded for its return trip to San Francisco. Today the 101 freeway enters San Rafael at this point, and the waterway, much shortened, is known as the San Rafael Canal. Pleasure craft and sailboats have replaced the hay scows. Courtesy, Bancroft Library

Reed's mill, which had fallen into disuse. After a short and successful operation, Barney moved to San Rafael where, as noted before, he became county judge in 1851 and served for seven years, after which he built a meat market with a business associate, Elisha DuBois.

Barney, a man with many talents, soon began the institution that would leave its indelible mark upon the history of San Rafael and Marin County. He summoned his bright and energetic son, Jerome, from New York, and with fatherly advice and money, established him as the first newspaper editor in the county. With both father and son sharing the burdens, the first issue of the *Marin County Journal* appeared on

Saturday, March 23, 1861, with paper manufactured at Samuel Penfield Taylor's paper mill in the redwood forests near Lagunitas Creek.

The weekly newspaper featured advertising for groceries, liquor, men's and women's clothing, livery stables, and for the San Rafael Institute and Boarding School run by Julia C. Gilbert. The *Journal* also published fiction, jokes, and sound moral advice for young men. Its early issues made an effort to reach what Jerome Barney called "the Hispanic-Americans," and he advised them that in the pages of "El Diario del Condado de Marin" (*The Marin County Journal*) the national news from the East, by way of the Pony Express, would appear in a bilingual column.

The masthead of the *Journal* stoutly declared that it was "Devoted to Foreign and Domestic News, Literature, Agriculture and the Interests of Marin County." The editorial in the second issue set the tone for the new paper:

. . . the *Journal* will be independent of clique, party or sect, doing justice to all and favor to none. Its chief aim will be

the encouragement of the resources of the county, especially its agricultural advantages and interests . . . We are satisfied that the county of Marin, with its great advantages and its favorable geographical position in relation to the great emporium on the Pacific [San Francisco] ought of right to occupy a front rank among the other counties of the State.

The objectivity of the *Journal* was tested early because, less than a month after its first issue, the Civil War began with the surrender of federal troops to the Confederacy at Fort Sumter, South Carolina, on April 13, 1861. The War divided Marin County along geographical lines with the coastal, lumber towns of the west strongly in favor of Abraham Lincoln and the preservation of the Union. In the 1860 election, Bolinas had voted for Lincoln 91 to 24, while in San Rafael the vote was 80 to 36 against him. The county as a whole barely gave the vote to Lincoln, and credit must be given to the *Journal* for its supportive role in these contentious times.

Twice in these years San Rafael was challenged for its position as the county seat. The geographical center of Marin was Nicasio, which, along with Novato, Olema, and Tomales, sent representatives to a convention in San Rafael on January 13, 1863, to resolve the matter since the governor had already authorized a bill allowing an election. When the ballots were counted, San Rafael had won easily, with 625 votes against removal and 290 votes for. A few years later, in 1866, the *Journal* reported another effort to supplant San Rafael, but no election was ever held.

The increasing importance of San Rafael was indicated not merely by the votes retaining it as the county seat, or even by the establishment of a weekly newspaper giving its citizens a forum for discussion and debate. What is perhaps more significant were the number of front-page advertisements in the *Journal* for San Francisco business establishments.

By the time the *Journal* was founded (1861), travel between San Rafael and San Francisco was common, if not always comfortable. As early as 1855, the steamer *Petaluma,* run by Captain Charles Mintern, was stopping at San Rafael as it plied the waters between San Francisco and the bustling port of Petaluma. By the early 1860s Bill Barnard's Stage Co. had San Rafael passengers waiting for the steamer's return from an overnight stop in Petaluma on its way back to San Francisco. The total cost of the trip was three dollars: two dollars to Captain Mintern and one

dollar to Bill Barnard. It is reported that the captain asked only once for the fare, and if you didn't have it, he looked the other way.

In 1915, James H. Wilkins, a former newspaper man, reminisced about these early days. His father, Hepburn Wilkins, was a wealthy San Francisco attorney who discovered the delights of San Rafael in 1863 and moved his family there. According to James Wilkins, his father was the first commuter between San Rafael and San Francisco:

The regular daily run began, if I recollect right, in April, 1864. The $3.00 single fare was not disturbed, but my father arranged for a commuted rate for himself of $50.00 per month ... As my father was the first who attempted to reside in Marin county and do business in San Francisco, so he was for some months the sole holder of a commutation ticket. When I see the immense throngs that cross the ferry

to and from Marin, commuters by the thousands, I always think of the time when there was only one.

These accounts of business and building, and of commerce and commuting, may give the impression that Yankee San Rafael was a sober and humorless place in the decades following the admission of California to the Union. Nothing could be further from the truth. Though the land belonged to the Yankees, the atmosphere was still that of "the days of the dons." As James Wilkins noted, "Over the whole country still hung the hazy, delightful flavor of Spanish-American romance." The hospitality of the ranchos was still strong, and "open houses" were in the best tradition with whole families on horseback visiting their neighbors on Sundays.

To capture the spirit of people at play, one must turn to "San Rafael Day," which changed every October 24 (then the feast of St. Rafael Arcangel) into a holiday of horseback riding and rope magic. Thomas Woods of Tomales was so expert in his riding and lariat throwing that he earned the title of "Tom Vaquero," itself a tribute to the superior horsemanship of the *Californios*. Later, in the mid-1860s, horsemanship was replaced by horse races, with ample betting on local favorites. Other forms of gambling included faro, monte, chuck-a-luck, red and white, rondo, and twenty-one. The bars were always full, and the saloons open all night.

As new wealth sprang up in San Francisco because of the Gold Rush, it needed an outlet for pleasure and entertainment. San Rafael Day provided it. In anticipation of the crowds coming by boat from across the bay, Angelo Angellotti, owner of the Marin Hotel, advertised in the pages of the *Journal* that the annual ball would be held in his hotel. With the sightseers came also the gamblers, thieves, and pickpockets from the Barbary Coast, whom the *Journal* called a "cut-throat, villaineous looking lot."

The main event of the day was a bull fight, which was well-advertised in advance to draw the crowds. The "Plaza de Torros" was set up near Second and B streets. And while the *matadors* and *picadores* in the early Mission days made one think briefly of Mexico City or Madrid, the event later degenerated into little more than a tired bull, or buck deer, being chased by young toughs eager to display their bravado.

In 1871 San Rafael Day had taken on a decidedly Yankee flavor, and an October issue of the *Journal* in that year noted:

Next Thursday is to be observed for the patron saint of San Rafael. We note arrangements are on foot for commemorating the day in a way more in accord with a Christian civilization than bull fighting and horse racing. It is proposed to have a barbecue and, evidently, a political discussion with able speakers for Grant and Greeley.

The disciples of Terpichore can choose between the pleasant hall over Anderson and duBios Market and the skating rink, indulge in the dreamy waltz or light quadrille.

In 1893, the city of San Rafael outlawed San Rafael Day because of the lawlessness and disorders it created, and, except for some brief revivals in the twentieth century, it has passed into oblivion.

The more farsighted visitors to San Rafael in those times discovered more than the high jinks of a bad bullfight and a sometimes rowdy crowd. As they looked about the growing town, they could see the signs of progress in the subdivision opened in 1857 by Alexander Forbes, and by the first telegraph message received in September 1863. Later that year, the first telegraph office opened, and San Rafael had instant communication with the outside world. The days of the Pony Express were over.

In 1864 Bill Barnard had added a twenty-passenger stagecoach on the run to San Quentin, and the next year bonds were floated so a toll road could be built, which cut a full hour off the commute from San Rafael to San Francisco. Bill Barnard reduced his fare by half, and the commuters kept coming. By March 1866 they could read in the pages of the *Journal* of how the town had changed:

> When we first became a resident, nearly fifteen years ago, San Rafael boasted of ten houses, besides the Mission buildings, one store, one boarding house and one whisky mill . . . Now we have three stores, two hotels, two boarding houses, one restaurant, two livery stables, public school, an academy, a newspaper, telegraph office, three bootmakers, two blacksmith shops, one harnessmaker, butcher shop, clockmaker, barber, three lawyers, a physician . . .

The previous years had seen slow and steady growth; the following years would witness a quickening of the pace of change. It was the age of the railroad and San Rafael wanted to be part of the future. The natural place for a transit was between San Rafael and the San Quentin ferry stop. A mass meeting on January 12, 1869, was held at Timothy Murphy's old adobe courthouse and $50,000 of capital stock was raised, to be divided into five hundred shares of $100 each. The next month the stockholders adopted a name for their railroad—The San Rafael and San Quentin Railroad—and elected directors: Adolph Mailliard (President), Sidney V. Smith, J.D. Walker, P.K. Austin, Jacob Short, James Ross, and L.A. Hinman.

The Chinese "coolies" in work gangs began to drive the piles for the new railroad, and the first trip was made on March 21, 1870. It took eight minutes to go from San Rafael to San Quentin, and the train made three trips daily with a "two-bit" (25 cent) fare.

An editorial writer, probably Jerome Barney, in the *Marin Journal* of April 16, 1870, could compare the "coaches and lumbering mud wagons" of an earlier day and the interminable delays between stagecoach and steamer, with the new railroad: "Now we trip down to the depot, a short distance from the hotels, wait on the platform a few minutes for the last tap of the bell, step into an elegant car, and in eight or ten minutes step off the car on to the steamer."

San Rafael and San Francisco in the past had been connected by Miwok tule-reed boats, Spanish sailing vessels, and Yankee schooners by water, then by horses and stagecoaches by land. The new link between them would be forged by the ferry boat and the railroad. The new forms of transportation were both handsome and expensive, seeming to require passengers equally so. And the passengers came. San Rafael was entering the Gilded Age.

Facing page: The Methodist Church of San Rafael—dedicated on February 18, 1870—is pictured in this early 1870s photo at Fifth Avenue between A and B streets. Later it was moved to 4th Street, where, in the fire of 1957, it was destroyed. The photo also shows the two-story B Street School at left center, and in the distance the handsome, white O'Connor home on Mission Avenue. The philanthropist A.W. Foster purchased the home and gave it to the Mount Tamalpais Military Academy. It still stands and is today called Foster Hall. Courtesy, Bancroft Library

Above, left: San Quentin Point is shown in this early photo, probably taken in the late 1860s before the formation of the San Rafael and San Quentin Railroad, which began service from San Rafael to Point San Quentin in 1870. Note the ferry smokestack at upper left. Captain Charles Mintern's ferry met passengers arriving at the Point three times daily. Before 1870 they traveled there on Bill Barnard's stagecoach; in later years ferry passengers arrived more comfortably on the railroad. By 1884 when the Union Station was built in San Rafael, the ferries no longer stopped at San Quentin, but rather at Tiburon, and Point San Quentin fell into disuse. Courtesy, Marin County Historical Society

CHAPTER 6
SAN RAFAEL IN THE GILDED AGE

The second half of the nineteenth century belonged to the West. It was the time of the realization of "Manifest Destiny," the territorial achievement of one nation "from sea to shining sea." With the dramatic discovery of gold at Sutter's Fort, the largest internal migration in U.S. history sent hundreds of thousands of Americans to California by foot, horse, wagon and, finally, by rail. These decades witnessed a change from the lawlessness of frontier life to the settled habits and manners of a new merchant class. It was a time both for vision and accomplishment, of vast undertakings, material progress, and social refinement.

Nowhere can this transition be better seen than in the career of William T. Coleman, known equally as "The Lion of the Vigilantes" for his role in ending crime and violence on the San Francisco waterfront and as the community leader whose first initiatives assured a more progressive and beautiful San Rafael. He typifies the wealthy San Franciscan who first came to San Rafael as a visitor, then returned to protect its natural charm and scenery, all the while opening it up for others as both residence and center of commerce.

William T. Coleman was a successful commission merchant who owned a fleet of clipper ships on the run

from New York to San Francisco. He was in the export market and introduced many California products to the East, from salmon and raisins to wine. His offices were found in major ports of the world, and his fame extended far beyond California. In 1888 he was seriously considered as a rival to President Grover Cleveland for the Democratic presidential nomination. Easterners admired his business acumen and clear thinking, yet the nomination was not offered, and Cleveland lost the election to General Benjamin Harrison.

Facing page: Short's Hall was built on the southeast corner of Fourth and C streets in the early 1860s by J.O.B. Short, a Kentucky native who came to San Rafael in 1847. Later a second story was added. It was here, on April 9, 1874, that the first meeting of the San Rafael Board of Trustees (later the City Council) was held. The first floor of the building was a saloon run by Archie McAllister, and San Rafael's first post office was located here. This 1870s photo shows both Short (with cane) and McAllister (in white) standing in front of the building. Courtesy, Marin County Historical Society

Above: William T. Coleman was a true patron of San Rafael. He lent his name, reputation, and money for the general improvement of the city. He was responsible for many civic projects, including parks and gardens, water works and recreation, homes and railroads, and schools and a library. Courtesy, Bancroft Library

Despite his fame in trade and business and his influence in large cities, Coleman was a man much attracted to nature and the environment. In 1916 Charles Lauff looked back to remember him:

He appeared to love Marin County and its green hills and valleys and spent his leisure hours tramping the hills and hunting deer. The valley of San Rafael was spread out before him in all its native loveliness, and the Mission San Rafael with its red tile roof like a brilliant ruby, surrounded by garnets, emeralds and sparkling gems. Was it any wonder that W. T. Coleman fell in love with this natural paradise and returned to purchase thousands of acres and to lay the foundation for the future of the city of San Rafael?

It was in 1871 that Coleman began to lay that foundation. In that year he purchased 1,100 acres on San Rafael's east side from Oliver Irwin for $84,000. The old Forbes tract was added and the total acreage was known as "Coleman's Addition." He then hired the eminent civil engineer Hammond Hall from San Francisco's Golden Gate Park to lay out the subdivision with lots ranging from one to twenty acres. His own nursery was twelve acres, and he imported eu-

calyptus trees from Australia to adorn the flatlands. He invited the famous landscape architect Frederick Law Olmsted to plan the formal gardens and he also retained local nurserymen like Italian immigrant John Zappatini to plant the trees and flowers. But gardens need water, and so, one year later, Coleman established the Marin County Water Company by purchasing the riparian rights on Lagunitas Creek from Adolph Mailliard. Though others formed the corporation with him, Coleman was the principal stockholder.

Enterprises like those were proof of the qualities that Charles Lauff remembered: "He was one of the

---

Above: The Shooting Star *was one of William T. Coleman's clipper ships that ran from New York to San Francisco. Coleman's sailing vessels of the late-nineteenth century were matched in the early twentieth century by the steamships of Robert Dollar. The maritime and mercantile success of Coleman and Dollar lent added splendor to the city in which they chose to live—San Rafael. Courtesy, The California Historical Society and* Marin Independent Journal

Facing page: The interior of Gardner's Candy Store, which stood on B Street between Third and Fourth. Courtesy, Marin County Historical Society

live men of the days of gold in San Francisco, and he never let grass grow under his feet, but grasped every opportunity that arose."

Coleman's role in the development of San Rafael was more than commercial. He also gave early residents an example of public service. By this time the county badly needed a courthouse, for the meetings were still held in what was left of Timothy Murphy's once-grand two-story adobe house, now in such disrepair that it was called "Murphy's mudpile." The time was ripe for enlightened civic action. Not surprisingly, on March 26, 1872, when Charles A. Parson, Thomas Ables, and William Barnard (the three Marin County supervisors) floated bonds to build a new courthouse, the name of W. T. Coleman appeared with several others to guarantee money for the county in the event of a deficit. Shortly thereafter, "Murphy's mudpile" was torn down, with Isaac Shaver paying $50 for the remaining redwood timbers.

The establishment of a new county courthouse marked an important period in the life of San Rafael and Marin County. In place of the old Mission buildings of an earlier day a Greek revival style building with a temple facade featuring large Corinthian columns was to arise. The architectural firm of Kenitzer and Raun, who had earlier designed the Charles Crocker mansion on San Francisco's Nob Hill, won the contract. Despite its elegance, the new structure would also be useful. Not only was a jail included, but the high entrance hall would be suitable for public hangings. If the new mood of San Rafael was progressive and enlightened, its leaders knew also that order was required.

San Rafael had never been far from signs of disorder, for the San Quentin prison was established nearby in 1854. Each new improvement in the town, from the water system at Lagunitas to new businesses advertising work clothes and groceries in the pages of the *Marin Journal,* meant that the convicts, like the citizens, were recipients of such services. For their part, they provided manual labor in building county roads, erecting homes, and even building hotels, like the Marin

Hotel. They were craftsmen, too, making furniture to sell to San Rafael residents.

Sometimes there was a jailbreak, as in 1862 when hundreds of prisoners escaped taking along the warden, John F. Challis, who was also the lieutenant governor of California. They moved up the Corte Madera Creek toward Ross Landing until they were headed off by a posse led by Sheriff Valentine Doub. It is reported that seven were killed and thirty taken prisoner, and the lieutenant governor was released. The rumor was that the convicts were going to sack San Rafael.

So, the high entrance hall in Marin County's new courthouse was a necessary feature because the hangings of San Quentin were actually done there, until 1893 when the prison itself became the site.

On August 1, 1872, the courthouse cornerstone was laid, and John Dwinelle, the man who one year before had spoken at the dedication of the San Francisco City Hall, was invited to give the formal oration. In his speech he spoke of the citizens "responding to the high instinct of civilization," and he compared the handsome new building with the very grandeur and stability of Mt. Tamalpais. To complete the sense of enlighten-

ment in the community, the new structure was the first public building to be equipped with gas lights.

Marin county was honored in having its own courthouse. San Rafael, the county seat, achieved a new prominence, which attracted people, commerce, and transportation. Yet farsighted men like William T. Coleman perceived that the town also needed regular city services for its own residents. On February 18, 1874, Governor Newton Booth signed Assembly Bill 90 into law, providing for the incorporation of San Rafael which embraced 160 acres centered on Fourth and B streets. Two months later, on April 6, 1874, the citizens—estimated to be 600 in number—turned out to elect a five-man board of trustees, the counterparts of today's city council. One hundred years later, the Marin County Historical Society would note: "William T. Coleman gave San Rafael the impetus that resulted in incorporation. For that reason, we honor him."

The first elected trustees were Sidney V. Smith, Joseph B. Rice, Sr., Dr. Alfred W. Taliaferro, William J. Miller, and Jacob Short, with Taliaferro receiving the most votes, 176. Hepburn Wilkins, the

first commuter from San Francisco who had by then become a full-time resident, was named the first town clerk at a salary of $300 per year. San Rafael's first town council was held in Short's Hall in the second story, but the next year moved into a new town hall, built, by Isaac Shaver, over a saloon. The council recommended the levying of a property tax and ordered a town survey by Hiram Austin, whose low bid of $175 won the day.

Later that year, on December 3, 1874, the trustees voted to form the San Rafael volunteer fire department. First known as the San Rafael Hose Company, it shortly changed its name to the San Rafael Hook, Ladder and Hose Company #1, and was given $1,000 to purchase fire-fighting equipment, which was housed on the first floor of Shaver's town hall. It is a remarkable tribute that for almost 75 years the head of the fire department received no pay. In 1945, Fred Scheuer, with over thirty years of volunteer service, was named San Rafael's first paid fire chief.

Fire was the most threatening hazard in a time when all structures were constructed of wood. It was the most important civic service, and even before street lights and paved roads were developed, the fire department was formed. An early account tells of its problems: In the spring of 1875, just months after the volunteers were organized, Bill Barnard's livery stables caught fire in a rain that caused the streets to become slippery and almost impassable. The fire wagon became mired in mud until strong hands and backs, with the help of horses, pushed and pulled it out. Finally arriving at the fire, the volunteers discovered there was no wrench to attach the hose. After retrieving a wrench, they discovered their hose was only 100 feet long, too short to reach the blaze. Disconsolate, the volunteers watched the stables burn to the ground. At the next town council meeting, approval was speedily given for the purchase of an additional hundred feet of hose.

Though primitive at the beginning, town services were expanded. As early as 1871, San Rafael had a small gas service organized by Allan Lee and J.O. Eldridge. The plant was not completed until 1875 when they won the franchise to service the newly incorporated town and installed the first street gas lights. In 1887, when electric lights replaced gas ones, Lee was named president of the San Rafael Gas and Electric Company. Telephone service was installed in 1879 with short, private lines established between doc-

tor's offices, though by 1884 service was extended to the public with one telephone connected to a long-distance line to San Francisco.

San Rafael's incorporation and the development of the town's services was a signal for further progress, not only in improving the lives of its citizens but in making its attractions known to a wider public. And San Rafael was not averse to advertising itself. One brochure of the time speaks of "The Sanatorium of

---

Facing page: The San Rafael Fire Department is pictured in this turn-of-the-century photo outside the station house on C Street between Fourth Street and Fifth Avenue. The driver is Sabin Kane and his brother Captain William Kane is seated beside him with Fred Williams standing in the rear. The two white horses were called "Tom and Jerry." In the buckboard behind are Chief Dan Schneider and Assistant Chief Walter Castro. Courtesy, Marin County Historical Society

Above: Ambrose Bierce, the short story writer, satirist, and wit, married Mary Ellen Day on Christmas Day 1871, and moved with his bride to 814 E Street in San Rafael where they lived for two years. He was a frequent ferry commuter to San Francisco and was known for taking solitary walks throughout the city. Bierce disappeared into Mexico in 1913 and was never heard of again. Portrait by Douglas Crane. Courtesy, Stanford University Library, Special Collections, and the Marin Independent Journal

San Rafael," pointing out that the town was not only protected from the coastal fogs by Mt. Tamalpais but secure also from Pacific Ocean winds retarded by a series of western hills that allowed only "balmy breezes" to reach it. Another pamphlet, in a section entitled, "Why San Rafael is Liked," stated that "take it all in all San Rafael affords more delightful residence sites than any other place in California with which we are acquainted, and we have traveled over a goodly portion of the state." The famous national magazine, *Harper's Weekly,* on May 29, 1875, featured six lithographs of San Rafael and nearby views entitled "The Suburbs of San Francisco."

Clearly San Rafael was admired. The problem was its accessibility. The San Rafael and San Quentin Railroad had been one answer, and a successful one both commercially and in terms of safety, for there had not been a single major accident. In 1869, the year the San Rafael railroad was begun, the Central Pacific Railroad had opened the great transcontinental road linking Eastern markets with Western produce. Whether across vast plains or in tying together local regions, the railroads had now become the chief means for developing both towns and trade.

In the late 1860s "railroad fever" hit Marin County, one sign of which was the formation of the Sausalito Land and Ferry Company. Purchasing 1,200 acres near Sausalito, the promoters offered 2,500 shares of

stock for sale at $500, with payments as low as $30 down and $15 per month. They also proposed a rail-road line all the way to Humboldt County. Homesites were widely advertised, and there was much talk of a "great city." But skepticism remained, and little came of the venture. The *Marin Journal* noted wryly: "New Sausalito is emphatically a big thing—on paper."

But other efforts were more successful. On December 16, 1871, the San Francisco and North Pacific Coast Railroad was formed by men with considerable lumber and land interests in western Marin County and along the Russian River in Sonoma County. They wanted a railroad between their redwood timber and the San Francisco housing boom, that would run from Sausalito through San Rafael, then northwest to To-males and beyond. To secure the necessary capital, they solicited subsidies from the many towns along the way. James McMillan Shafter of Point Reyes, and Austin D. Moore, the latter of whom owned half interest in the Russian River Land and Lumber Company, and others urged Marin citizens to support the new "narrow gauge" railroad. Arthur Moore was a persuasive public relations man, and he pointed out the economic advantages of a "narrow gauge" rail line, which

allowed a width of no more than three feet between rails.

In 1872 the citizens responded, voting 482 to 228 in favor. The board of supervisors promptly awarded a subsidy of $160,000 to the North Pacific Coast Railroad. Disagreements quickly arose, however, when the

Facing page, top: The view looking southeast from San Rafael Hill to San Quentin Point is shown in this turn-of-the-century photo. Note the Union Station at right near center. Just behind it is the San Rafael Canal. The line of trees in the upper right indicates the San Quentin Toll Road, which is today's Francisco Boulevard. Courtesy, Bancroft Library

Facing page, bottom: This unusual photo of the late 1870s looks eastward and shows the broad avenues which we know today as Fifth Avenue (left) and Fourth Street (right). The fence in the right foreground marks the boundary of Zopf's Vineyard at to-day's Fourth and H streets, while in the distance, the cupola of the original Marin County Courthouse rises. Opposite the court-house is St. Rafael's Catholic Church. Courtesy, Bancroft Library

Above: This 1896 photo shows the little depot for the narrow-gauge railroad known as the B Street Station. It was below Second Street and behind the buildings on B Street. The tall building in the background is the Flat Iron Building. Horse-drawn carriages standing in water after a sudden rain are awaiting the passengers. Courtesy, Marin County Historical Society

supervisors learned that San Rafael would not be on the main line. Citing heavy costs in cutting either through the ridge south of San Rafael or north to Tomales through White's Hill, the engineers decided that a route through Ross Valley would be more economical. As a result, San Anselmo would serve as "The Junction" of the new railroad, not San Rafael, which would be reduced to a mere spur.

The controversy over the route finally ended with the supervisors approving the change in direction, though men like William T. Coleman fought with lawsuits every step of the way. Finally, on January 7, 1875, the North Pacific Coast Railroad was formally opened. In the same year, it acquired the old San Rafael and San Quentin Railroad, changing its tracks to narrow gauge. San Francisco passengers to San Rafael now had an option: they could disembark at Sausalito for a pleasant train ride through the wooded Ross Valley to the San Anselmo junction and the spur to San Rafael, or they could take the paddle-wheeled

ferry to Point San Quentin and the short, three-mile train ride directly to town.

But San Rafael was still off the main line and many citizens didn't like it. The man who was to give San Rafael its own line, the powerful Peter Donahue, had already brought his San Francisco and North Pacific Railroad into adjoining Sonoma County, linking Petaluma with Santa Rosa and points north. Donahue was a machinist from Scotland who discovered that building foundries was more lucrative than the search for gold; his advantage lay in his ability to provide his own machines and engines in competitive local bidding. Earlier he had expanded his broad-gauged railroad from Petaluma to San Rafael. The dream of a direct link south from San Rafael was realized in 1884 when Donahue pushed his line through several tunnels to Tiburon, where he inaugurated a new ferry service to San Francisco. In the process, Donahue created the town of Tiburon.

For the next fifteen years the two railroads were rivals for the San Francisco passenger trade, with each company advertising lower rates and more tourist attractions. The race between them extended even to their ferry boats, with Donahue's *Tiburon* leaving that terminal, while the North Pacific Coast's *San Rafael* moved out from Sausalito, both headed for San Francisco's Ferry Building. Observers say the *San Rafael* usually won. The people of San Francisco responded by the thousands, and a weekend in Marin County was a fine vacation for those living in that fog-enshrouded city. Many liked what they saw and stayed. From a mere 600 persons in 1874, the population of San Rafael grew to 2,276 residents by 1880.

The story of Marin's railroads would be incomplete without mention of the men who actually built them, the men who cleared the land, planted the dynamite, and laid the tracks. They were the unskilled laborers,

usually Irish or Chinese. Some railroad men, like Peter Donahue, would not hire the Chinese. As Donahue stated, "Everything I ever got in this country I got out of the bone and sinews of white men." But with the completion of the railroads, hundreds of workers—whether Asian or Caucasian—were out of work.

Many of the unemployed Chinese moved to Point San Pedro—today's China Camp—where they set up villages near the off-shore shrimp beds. Harvesting the shrimp and exporting it to China was a fair substitute for work on the railroads. Yet discrimination pursued them in the form of state laws limiting their fishing rights or denying them altogether, and in 1882 the U.S. Congress passed the Chinese Exclusion Act, which prohibited further Chinese immigration. In 1886 an Anti-Chinese League was formed in San Rafael, with the aim of expelling the Chinese from California and boycotting local businesses who employed them.

An 1880 account notes that 225 Chinese occupied land owned by John F. McNear, who had established a small steamship line on Point San Pedro near today's McNear's Beach for trade with both Petaluma and San Francisco. McNear leased the land to Richard Bullis for $1,000, and Bullis promptly leased it to the Chinese for almost $3,000.

Facing page, top: The ferryboat San Rafael *was built for the North Pacific Coast Railroad in 1877 for service between Sausalito and San Francisco. It claimed the record for this passage at 17 minutes. On one foggy night—November 30, 1901—the* San Rafael *pulled out from the Ferry Building in San Francisco heading for Sausalito. The ferryboat* Sausalito, *heading for San Francisco, met the* San Rafael *just off Alcatraz and ploughed into her side. The* San Rafael *sank in 20 minutes with the loss of two lives. Courtesy, Marin County Historical Society*

Facing page, bottom: The San Rafael *commuters in this late-1880s photo include H.L. Sweeney, president of the Hotel Rafael Co., and banker William Babcock standing on the left side. They had returned from San Francisco on Peter Donohue's ferryboat* Tiburon *where, at Tiburon, they were met by the San Francisco and North Coast train for the ride to San Rafael, thence by horse and carriage to their homes. Courtesy, Bancroft Library*

Top, right: China Camp lies on the north side of Point San Pedro facing San Pablo Bay. This 1889 photo shows the housing and piers used by the Chinese shrimp fisherman as well as a large number of shrimp drying in the sun (center). The Chinese were the chief shrimp fishermen in California, though laws limiting their activities were frequently passed by the state legislature. Today China Camp is a state park. Courtesy, Ann T. Kent California Room, Marin County Library

The great variety of ethnic groups in Marin County is recorded in the register of voters in 1880. Of the 1,621 voters, 273 were from Ireland, 101 from Germany, 90 from Switzerland, and 62 from Portugal, followed by English, Canadian, and French. All of these were men, since women did not have the vote. In San Rafael itself, of the 619 registered voters, 128 were Irishmen, most of whom were railroad workers.

With the completion of the railroads, San Rafael became a mecca for the wealthy, who found there more and more of the amenities associated with a fashionable resort town. Arriving in San Rafael, the visitor could find accommodations at the Marin Hotel, or the Albion. In 1870 the grand Tamalpais Hotel opened and, at $15 per night, catered to more expensive tastes. The largest and most elegant hotel of all, the Hotel Rafael, was opened on June 4, 1888. It was located on "Coleman's Addition," not far from where Dominican College stands today. With 101 rooms, an observation tower, clubhouse, barroom, card rooms, billiard tables, bowling alleys, cottages, tennis courts, stables, and large landscaped gardens, the Hotel Rafael was easily the largest and most select resort hotel in the North Bay.

The Hotel Rafael's stockholders were a "Who's Who" of San Rafael aristocracy. They included, besides William T. Coleman, James Mervyn Donahue, the son of Peter Donahue, who lived in a commodious mansion on today's Lincoln Avenue built for him by his father, and whose sister married J.H. Von Schroeder, a German, who managed the hotel; William Babcock, a banker and tugboat tycoon who built the San Rafael showplace called "Edgehill" in 1882; and A.W. Foster, who in 1880 bought Adolph Mailliards's 135-acre estate, including the mansion, vineyards, and orchards, and named it "Fairhills."

The cultural life of San Rafael expanded in 1879 when Upton M. Gordon financed and built an opera house. With Anson P. Hotaling, his silent partner, Gordon had already built the first bank building in 1871 and established the town's first banking institution, Gordon's Bank. When he erected the opera house, which also served as the community's assembly hall, he placed it next door to the bank, a further sign that culture and commerce were never far apart in the San Rafael of the Gilded Age.

As important as railroads, homes, hotels, and opera houses were in attracting people to San Rafael, other institutions were even more essential. In the April 17, 1873, edition of the *Marin Journal,* a meeting of the San Rafael School District was reported, which included the remarks of William T. Coleman: "Schools more than anything else attract good people to a place. Men coming to a place ask 'where are your schools? where are your churches? where are your means of

---

Facing page: The elegant Hotel Rafael was built in 1887 and opened in 1888. The five-story structure cost $200,000. It was located on 21 acres in "Coleman's Addition" in today's Dominican College area. It flourished during the railroad era when families spent entire summer seasons there. During the 1918 flu epidemic, it was used as an emergency hospital. On July 29, 1928, an arsonist set it ablaze (bottom photo) and it was destroyed in two hours. Courtesy, Bancroft Library

The San Rafael Brewery, photographed in the late 1890s. Courtesy, Marin County Historical Society

communication?' but always first, 'where are your schools?'" The *Journal* added, "His remarks were received with prolonged applause."

Credit for the first public school usually goes to the San Rafael Institute, directed by Julia Gilbert, a graduate of the Kalamazoo Female Seminary in Michigan. First a private institution, the Institute became a public school in 1861 along with another founded by her father, the Rev. Harvey Gilbert of the Southern Baptist Church. As early as 1859, Rev. Gilbert was instrumental in securing donations and land to build a school

which was approved by the town trustees and named the Gilbert School. In 1862, John Simms, the first elected county superintendent of schools, donated land and built a school at the corner of Fifth and B streets, which was removed in 1871 to make way for a new two-story classroom building that cost $4,500.

Some students attended private schools. In 1866 Professor Charles Miel opened the Young Ladies Seminary. In 1882 the Selbourne School was opened by William Bates, to become the Hitchcock Academy in 1898 after being renamed for the Episcopal priest

who replaced him. The Mt. Tamalpais Military Academy was organized in 1890, and two years later moved to the Tamalpais Hotel under the direction of the Presbyterian minister, the Rev. Arthur Crosby, who resigned his pulpit for the new position.

Dominican College came to San Rafael in 1888 when the Dominican nuns abandoned their school in Benicia, which had been in operation since 1854. With the approval of San Francisco Archbishop Riordan, they purchased twenty acres from William T. Coleman at a cost of $20,000, though half that sum was remitted back as a gift and the other half taken out as a loan. The site was "Coleman's Addition," not far from the Hotel Rafael and close to the residences of families who would send their daughters to the nuns for elementary and secondary education. In 1889 a four-story Victorian Italianate-style building was completed as a motherhouse for the nuns and as a boarding school. The success of Dominican College, which became a four-year college in 1917, may be measured by its acquisition of William Babcock's "Edgehill" in 1920 and the purchase in 1918 of "Meadowlands," which had been built in 1889 by Michael de Young, the founder of the *San Francisco Chronicle.*

Besides having a choice of good schools, the visitor to San Rafael could worship at the church of his choice. The Presbyterian Church had been active since 1869 and by 1876 had its own church building under the pastorate of the Rev. James McDonald. Its influence was extended further through the San Francisco Theological Seminary, which was moved from San Francisco to San Anselmo in 1891 when A. W. Foster donated a 17-acre site. The Methodist Church was also a pioneer church, which held services for a time in Timothy Murphy's adobe house and by 1871 had erected its own house of worship. St. Paul's Episcopal Church under the Rev. William H. Dyer received the support of Mr. and Mrs. John D. Walker and other Anglicans, who built a redwood church in 1870.

By the 1890s in San Rafael, there was a sense of gracious living among the large tracts of homes, gardens and trees, an ample and growing downtown center of diversified business, public and private schools, libraries, churches and cultural institutions, municipal services, and two fine railroad and ferry systems linking all of Marin County to San Francisco and points north. The Town Improvement Society was

formed in 1887 to maintain and enlarge the attractive conditions. In addition, San Rafael could note with pride the twin civic satisfactions of being the county seat with a classical courthouse and being an incorporated town in its own right.

Best of all, San Rafael had not yet "boomed," as one publication put it, still retaining its country charm and rustic allure, which kept weekend visitors coming over from the big city across the bay.

The year 1893 might be called the apex of San Rafael's Gilded Age for in that year two events occurred, one that looked backward, the other forward. William T. Coleman had invested heavily in borax deposits in southern California, a mineral protected by tariffs. After President Cleveland's election in 1888, a bill he signed removed borax from the tariff list. This single act ruined Coleman and sent him into bankruptcy. Though he paid off his creditors, the disaster took its toll on his health. He died November 22, 1893. In the same year, San Rafael reached 3,500 residents, an achievement that entitled it to become a city of the "fifth class" (fifth most populous in the state).

The death of William T. Coleman marked the end of an era, while the change of San Rafael from a town to a city portended an urban future in which the automobile would replace the railroad, and bridges would replace the ferry. It was a future that the citizens anticipated, for in 1898 "The Ten Thousand Club," a booster organization dedicated to increasing the population of the city to 10,000 by the year 1900, was begun. San Rafael was entering the twentieth century with confidence and pride.

Facing page: The San Rafael Junior Tennis Club from the Bates School, photographed in 1889. Courtesy, Marin County Historical Society

Above: Bicycling gained popularity as a leisure activity in San Rafael during the late-nineteenth century. These men are members of the San Rafael Wheelmen, photographed in 1896. Courtesy, Marin County Historical Society

CHAPTER 7
THE EARLY TWENTIETH CENTURY

By 1900 the work of the San Rafael pioneers was all but completed. The pastures of the Mission were gone, and the Mexican land grants were no longer intact. In their place was a quiet retreat of large homes and a modest business district with outlying towns laced together by the railroad, while the grand hillside mansions were visited by the horse-drawn phaetons or carriages. Though there was some local industry associated with the railroads, the livery stables, and the lumberyards, the atmosphere of San Rafael was that of a gracious and sedate resort town whose inhabitants had succeeded in avoiding the bustle of San Francisco business and trade for the leisurely pursuits of bucolic, suburban life.

In the 1920s a character in a Gertrude Atherton novel exclaimed, "Oh, God, let me climb. Yank me up into the paradise of San Francisco Society, Burlingame, Alta, Menlo Park, Atherton, Belvedere, San Rafael." But if San Rafael was part of "the paradise of San Francisco Society," its residents required some of the amenities and comforts associated with such happiness, things like electric trains, city parks, hospitals.

Transportation has always been linked to progress, and nowhere is this more evident than in the development of San Rafael. And among forms of transporta-

tion, some are preferable to others. As early in the century as 1902, for example, petitions circulated to prevent the use of automobiles on the highways of Marin, and a law required them to stop when they met a horse. Even among the trains there had developed a distinction between the steam train for freight and the electric train for passengers. Cleaner and less noisy, the electric trains came to Marin in 1902 when the North Shore Railroad took over the North Pacific Railroad. By 1903 the first electric train between Sausalito and San Rafael, by way of San Anselmo, was operating. It was one of the first suburban electric train services in California, and it grew steadily. By 1914 there were accommodations for over 5,000 passengers in its fleet of cars.

The speed and comfort in reaching San Rafael was soon to be matched by a public destination worthy of the passengers. It was in 1905 that the City of San Rafael accepted the gift of Boyd Park and the Gate House from Louise Cook Boyd and John Franklin

---

Facing page: This 1909 photo looking eastward shows the busy thoroughfare that Fourth Street had become. Women in white dresses scurry across the unpaved street while automobiles and horse-drawn carriages compete for the right of way. Courtesy, Marin County Historical Society

Boyd to honor the memory of their sons Seth and John, who had died as teenagers. April 29, 1905, was a gala day when the presentation was made. Every business was closed, including the numerous saloons, and 4,000 people—the entire city population of the time—were in attendance.

The Gate House had been built in 1879 for Ira B. Cook, the grandfather of Louise Boyd, and it was among the most handsome homes of the era. The *Marin Journal* of October 16, 1879, called it "A magnificent improvement . . . unique and grand and when completed the place will be one of the most beautiful to be found on the coast." Today Ira B. Cook's Gothic Revival Gate House is the home and museum of the Marin County Historical Society, standing splendidly at the entrance to a playground and park of many wooded acres. As if these progressive events in the life of San Rafael were not sufficient signs of a community aiming to better itself, the early years of the century also witnessed the establishment of the San Rafael Improvement Club. The Club's agenda for action was wide, including tree planting, cleaning up the muddy conditions of Fourth Street during winter rains, and the elimination of the mosquito. With the canal now being dredged and with saltwater sloughs nearby, mosquitoes found many places to breed. G.W. Woodworth, a professor of entomology at the University of California (Berkeley), earned the gratitude of the Improvement Club by treating the surface of the tidal marshes with kerosene and oil. So prevalent and pesky was this offensive insect that a poem to commemorate it was composed by Dr. C.G. Buck, a later director of the Marin Mosquito Abatement District:

The San Rafael mosquito
He hangs around and sings all night
Sings all night, sings all night
Stops at times to take a bite
Then flies to Sausalito.

It is not surprising that the health of San Rafael citizens was, given the city's favorable climate and location, often taken for granted. Not until 1905 was

a hospital established, though long before that sanatoriums, as well as able medical doctors, existed. San Rafael's first doctor was A. W. Taliaferro, and no account of early medicine would be complete without acknowledging his pioneering service, extending from the date of California's statehood in 1850 to the year of his death, 1885. Taliaferro was a legend even in his own time and, though he lived in today's Fairfax, he made house calls throughout the county—especially in San Rafael where he enjoyed the social life, the card playing, the whiskey drinking, and keeping up with the events of the day. Taliaferro served in both state and county offices, and his name will never be forgotten. On his grave in San Rafael's Mt. Tamalpais Cemetery are engraved the words:

His Virtue was Generosity
His Friends a Legion
His Enemies None
One of Nature's Noblemen.

In 1895 two sisters, Therese and Adeline Smith, recent graduates of the California Women's Hospital School in San Francisco, began operating a sanatorium in the home of their mother Mrs. Robert Smith. In 1905 San Rafael's first hospital, the Cottage Hospital, was established at the corner of Fifth and Lincoln streets. The incorporation papers were signed by Dr. William Farrington Jones, H. O. Howitt, and William J. Wickman. The hospital survived and flourished for half a century, though its name was later changed to the San Rafael General Hospital.

Facing page: James Watson's saloon, photographed circa 1900. Courtesy, Marin County Historical Society

Above, left: In this 1880s photo of the newly completed Boyd Gate House, it appears beside its ornamental gardens with a view of downtown San Rafael behind. At this time it was known as part of the estate of Ira B. Cook and his sons, Seth and Dan. Today the iron fence remains at the end of Mission Avenue, and the Gate House contains the offices and museum of the Marin County Historical Society. Courtesy, Bancroft Library

Left: The San Rafael Improvement Club building was once part of the pavilion of the 1915 Panama-Pacific Exposition in San Francisco. It was relocated to the corner of Fifth Avenue and H Street in San Rafael where it stands today. In 1974, Rosemarie Arthur (left) and Erma Thaning (right) posed in Victorian dresses before the main entrance. Courtesy, Marin Independent Journal

It was perhaps providential that the Cottage Hospital was founded in 1905, one year before the San Francisco Earthquake.

The genteel tranquility of San Rafael was broken at 5:12 A.M. the morning of April 18, 1906, when the San Andreas fault shifted for a distance of over 250 miles leaving destruction, fire, and death in its wake. It measured 8.6 on the Richter Scale, and in one place, near Tomales, a fissure 21-feet deep opened in the earth. The fire that followed the earthquake caused most of the devastation, damage, hardship, and death.

After the earthquake, official estimates listed 478 persons dead and property damage amounted to $300 million dollars. Recent research, however, indicates that the number of dead was over 2,500 with damage exceeding one billion dollars in 1906 money.

San Rafael residents stood looking south to the billowing black smoke across the bay, and the following day they turned to the *Marin Journal* to read the headline: "FIRE FOLLOWS BIG EARTHQUAKE," while smaller headlines noted: "Tomales Demolished" and "Santa Rosa Ruined." Though relatively unscathed by the earthquake, San Rafael itself was indirectly affected in substantial ways.

In the next busy weeks, mass meetings were held and relief committees were formed. A huge camp was established behind the Rafael Hotel, and fifty tents were erected, with a 20-foot wooden shed constructed for dispensing meals. It was estimated that 250,000 people left San Francisco following the earthquake, and San Rafael received over 10,000 of the refugees. Over $12,000 dollars were contributed to the San Rafael Relief Committee and its sub-committees: Ladies Relief Committee, Police Committee, Finance Committee, Provisions Committee, and Shelter Committee.

Like earlier visitors, those who fled San Francisco in 1906 liked what they saw in San Rafael. One early record shows that the city's population leaped from 4,000 before the earthquake to 6,500 following it. Most visitors did not stay long, though the exodus did produce some new residents and some businesses transplanted from San Francisco.

One such firm was the Carson Glove Company, which almost immediately decided to rebuild its ruined industry in San Rafael, thereby bringing in 100 new jobs with the promise of 100 more. The citizens could congratulate themselves that a business with

$4,000 a month in payroll checks was to flourish in their midst.

Another refugee from San Francisco was an entrepreneur and boxer named Billy Shannon, whose training camp in San Francisco was also to become a new feature of San Rafael life. With his wife Ella, Shannon ran a bar and restaurant for the visitors who came to see boxers exhibit their skills in his small ring. Shannon was a former California state amateur lightweight champion whose friendly manner and business savvy made his camp attractive to many famous fighters of the day. World lightweight champions like Joe Gans and Willie Ritchie trained at Billy Shannon's Villa in the years immediately following the earthquake. Late in his life, at age 82, Willie Ritchie remembered San Rafael as "a warm and wonderful place to train."

Not everyone agreed that boxing was a good thing for San Rafael. An advertisement posted around town in early September 1908 tells of a mass meeting to be held in Boyd Memorial Park "to protest the passage of an ordinance legalizing prize-fighting in San Rafael." It closes with the stirring words: "Citizens, Attend and Do Your Duty. Women of San Rafael, Protect Your Homes!"

The presence of prize-fighting was not, however, incompatible with the pleasures of genteel and affluent

Facing page: Though the Marin County Medical Society was first formed in 1897, it was reconstituted in 1905. This photo, taken shortly thereafter, shows the membership: (front, l-r) Dr. John Keck, the Rev. Joseph Byrne (honorary member), Dr. A.G. Winn, Dr. S.M. Augustine, Dr. George Powers, Dr. Earnest D. Chipman, Dr. H.J. Crumpton; (center) Dr. H.W. Dudley, Dr. William Farrington Jones (founder), Dr. H.O. Howitt, Dr. J.H. Kuser, Dr. William J. Wickman, Dr. Arthur H. Mays; (back) Dr. Harry O. Hund, Dr. F.J. Hund, Dr. S.M. Alexander, Dr. F.E. Sawyer. Courtesy, Roy Farrington Jones and the Marin County Historical Society

Above, right: Donaldina Cameron and her wards were among those who sought refuge in San Rafael after the 1906 earthquake. Cameron rescued Chinese girls from brothel slavery and prostitution. She was called "Lo Mo," the Mother, and established the Chinese Presbyterian Mission Home on Sacramento Street in San Francisco; it was very active in San Rafael during the early decades of the twentieth century. This 1906 photo of Cameron (top row, second from left) with Chinese girls and small boys was taken at their new home on 3 Bayview Street in San Rafael. Courtesy, Ann T. Kent California Room, Marin County Library

living, nor with the acquisition of property by which such living is maintained. In the same year as the earthquake shipping magnate Robert Dollar purchased the Queen Anne-style Victorian mansion at the other end of the block from the Boyd Gate House. Built in 1888 for the widow Ella Park, the mansion was designed by architect Clinton Day, who also designed the famous "City of Paris" in San Francisco. The Dollar family had lived in San Rafael since 1892 and had been benefactors to the Presbyterian Orphanage in San Anselmo as well as to the San Francisco Theological Seminary. They named their new home "Falkirk" after Dollar's birthplace in Scotland. In 1974 the City of San Rafael acquired Falkirk, its lovely rooms, gardens, and greenhouse, and it is now known as the Falkirk Cultural Center.

While San Rafael in these times was the home of Robert Dollar, founder of the first round-the-world cruises which made the Dollar Steamship Co. internationally famous, it was also the scene of the humbler pursuits of ordinary people relaxing on the weekend, going swimming, or attending the movies.

Though the canal near Irwin Street had provided an open air swimming hole for many years, the newly-elected City Council in 1914 decided that something finer was required for the people of San Rafael. Accordingly, they voted $40,000 for the construction of a new, enclosed bathhouse to be built on the site of the old swimming hole. Many an aquacade was performed in what came to be known as the Municipal Bathhouse, and many fine swimmers, including the local girl, Eleanor Garatti, were developed there. Eleanor Garatti was the dominant woman swimmer of the late 1920s. In July 1928 she won the national 100-meter swimming championship at the Olympic trials at Rockaway Beach in New Jersey, breaking the world's record. Later, at the 1928 Amsterdam Olympics, she placed second in the 100-meter freestyle

competition, and was a member of the winning U.S. relay team. At one time, she held three world records.

Weekends in San Rafael in the early decades of the twentieth century also included taking in the silent films. The West had not yet cast off its romantic Spanish past, and movies about bandits, cowboy heroes, and damsels in distress required rustic backgrounds of scenic beauty. Marin County in 1910 was an agricultural region, ranking third among California counties in both egg and milk products. Of its 338,560 acres, 263,442 acres were farmland. Movie producers quickly saw the possibilities of locating a film company in San Rafael thus avoiding the extensive travel to be "on location." The Essanay Company came in 1911 and stayed for eight months, to be followed by the Argus Film Company in 1913 and the California Motion Picture Corporation in 1914.

The largest and most productive of the film companies was organized by producer George Middletown, who brought technicians, actresses, and actors from southern California to establish the Michelena Stu-

---

dios, honoring the star Beatriz Michelena. The films were built around famous stories of the day, including Bret Harte's "Salomey Jane" and "The Lily of Poverty Flat." The grand opera *Mignon* was filmed here with Miss Michelena in the starring role. A number of actors who later attained fame first appeared in San Rafael films, actors like Zasu Pitts, Jack Holt, Slim

Summerville, Leo Carrillo, and the great Otis Skinner. One of the movie industry's most famous directors, Frank Capra, gained his first film experience here.

Films set in the old Spanish days were very popular, and directors used local scenes, like A. W. Foster's great house and gardens, "Fairhills." Many prominent citizens of the town, men such as Judge Edward Butler and Sabin Kane (who later became chief of police) performed. Though the Michelena Film Studio did not last through the 1930s and the heyday of Hollywood, it provided the means for many thousands of people to see for the first time the beauty of San Rafael through the melodramas of the silent film era.

The sports and entertainment of the time, however, did not deter the people from seeking more permanent progress in the life of the community. One sign of that

progress was a city library, which the citizens had been planning for many years. The San Rafael Mechanics' Institute was incorporated in 1871, and a small library was erected in 1887, to be turned over to the town trustees in 1890. What was truly needed was a building with a grandeur and dignity to match the aspirations of the reading public. In 1904 the Good Government Club of San Rafael began the quest for a Carnegie endowment for a public library. Though delayed by the 1906 Earthquake, the effort finally succeeded, and the formal dedication of the San Rafael Public Library took place on January 14, 1909.

A personal friend of Andrew Carnegie, Judge Morrow, made the presentation, calling the library

"the people's university ... enabling anyone who avails himself of its services to stand on the shoulders of all the greatest thinkers of the past and reach a still higher degree of Knowledge." Judge F. M. Angellotti provided the local view of the importance of the new library by noting that the city had recently acquired a public park (Boyd's Memorial Park) and would soon move into a new city hall. By 1909 San Rafael had surrounded itself with the obvious signs of civic progress: a park, a library, a post office, and a city hall.

In the San Rafael of this time there was a mood of public confidence and self-determination—and the desire to have the city responsive to its own citizens rather than a remote state legislature. They sought a form of "home rule" whereby the people themselves would be the judge of community needs. In 1912 a fifteen-man board of freeholders was elected to write

Facing page, top: The cast of Argentine Love—*a movie filmed in San Rafael around 1915—is pictured above. Note the tall, handsome cowboy in black to the left of the seated figure, and, to the right, the lovely senorita. The film featured "Marin Sais and an all-star cast." Most movie themes of the period had a Spanish flavor or depicted the Gold Rush days of 1849. Courtesy, Marin County Historical Society*

Facing page, bottom: San Rafael's Victoria Theater, photographed circa 1910. Courtesy, Marin County Historical Society

Below: Mme F.J. Mazet's French Laundry was located at 407 D Street between Second and Third streets. In this 1907 photo she stands at the left with her family, while to her right her employees stand in front of the building. The delivery wagon and river are standing ready at the curb. Unpaved streets made laundries like Madam Mazet's quite popular. The structure was built and owned by Jean and Jeanne Dafau, another French family of San Rafael, who sold it to Mazet at the turn of the century. Courtesy, Marin County Historical Society

a city charter. Six months later, the voters approved the new charter to take effect in 1913. Among other changes, it provided that the mayor, city clerk, city attorney, and chief of police be elected directly by the people with no party designations. Edward Kinsella was the first elected mayor of San Rafael under the new charter.

In the next few years, with the onset of World War I, San Rafael would be abruptly shaken from its local concerns to become part of the national effort to win the war against the Kaiser. With Woodrow Wilson's declaration of war against Germany on April 6, 1917, the city mobilized for patriotic purposes. Company D, Fifth Infantry, of the National Guard of California, answered the call with 62 members enlisting within the first weeks. By June 200 men were ready for service, and in September the first contingent of soldiers for overseas assignment was assembled. Newspaper accounts tell of "the cheers of thousands ringing in their ears," as the new recruits marched toward the Union Depot preceded by the San Rafael High School Band, Eagle Drum Corps, the Fire Department,

Hitchcock Academy and Mt. Tamalpais Military Academy cadets, and followed by schoolchildren and many automobiles. Both the "Marseillaise" and "The Star Spangled Banner" were played.

Those who remained behind were not inactive, as people purchased Liberty Bonds to pay the costs of war. The allotment for San Rafael was $225,000, and a newspaper account stated that "it was exceeded by $11,000 and is still growing." Julia Babcock, William Babcock's wife, signed for $5,000 in Liberty Bonds, while the officers and guards at San Quentin signed for $20,000. Even the prisoners contributed $1,000.

In August 1918 the first war deaths from San Rafael were recorded in the local press: Frank Costa and Tony Morris. Later, Hepburn Wilkins II, the son of newspaperman James H. Wilkins, was killed in action. After the war, he was memorialized in the Wilkins Post of the American Legion.

Three days after the war's end (November 11, 1918) there was a parade down Fourth Street, which 5,000 people attended, followed by a ceremony lasting two hours. Local headlines read:

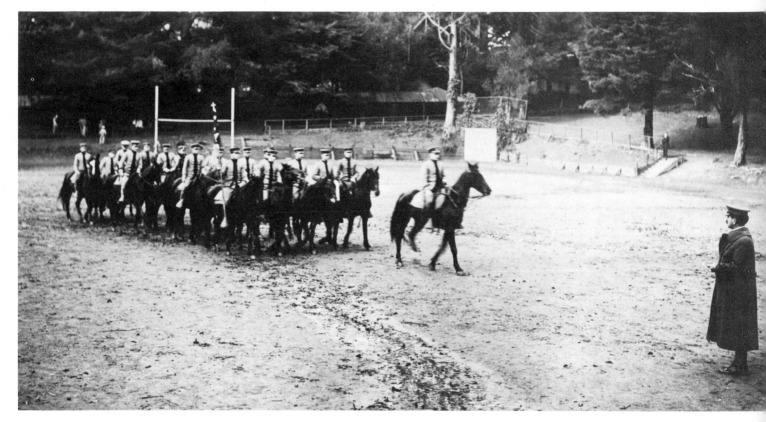

THOUSANDS CELEBRATE GERMANY'S
DOWNFALL
GREATEST PARADE IN HISTORY OF
SAN RAFAEL
MARKS SIGNING OF WAR ARMISTICE

In one respect World War I was beneficial to the health of the citizens of San Rafael. It was in 1918 that the influenza epidemic struck, and people were arrested for refusing to wear flu masks. Citing the need for a large facility to handle the many stricken people, authorities commandeered the splendid Hotel Rafael as a hospital. County Health Officer Dr. J. H. Kuser successfully argued that since the hotel belonged to Baron Von Schroeder who was then fighting with the German Army, the property could be taken over under the Alien Sedition Act. Red Cross volunteers and Dominican nuns assisted as nurses, and prominent people helped; Louise A. Boyd, the famous Arctic explorer, sent her chauffeur to downtown rooming houses to pick up the sick and transport them to the Hotel, now doubling as a hospital.

With natural disasters and a world war behind it, San Rafael welcomed the 1920s with a return to the gracious and leisurely ways of an earlier time. In 1920

Catherine and Florence Branson, graduates of Bryn Mawr, were invited to leave their teaching posts in the East to take charge of the San Rafael Girls' School, and in that same year Robert Dollar donated twelve acres to the Boyd Memorial Park. In 1921 the Hotel Rafael was recognized by the California Tennis Association as an official site for championship play, even though state championships had been held there since the late 1800s. Golfers found their exercise at the Marin Golf and Country Club, which had also been active since 1909, the year that a passenger boat with

Facing page: A San Rafael baseball team, photographed October 18, 1913. Top row (l-r): Cy Ross, Happy Hogan, Jim Ncalow, Al Barrow (manager), (unidentified), Babe Hollis; bottom: Rollie Totheroh, Craig Jorgensen, —Brundage, Vasco Andre. Courtesy, Marin County Historical Society

Above: The Mount Tamalpais Military Academy was organized in 1890 and took over the old Tamalpais Hotel in 1892 when Presbyterian minister Arthur Crosby became the headmaster. Its last graduation exercises were held in 1925, though it continued in existence as the San Rafael Military Academy until 1971. In this World War I-period photo, mounted cadets pass in review on the parade grounds. Courtesy, Marin County Historical Society

a capacity of 65 people was chartered to run between San Rafael and the Club, which was then located between the city and McNear's Point.

The 1920s also witnessed the coming of Prohibition with the ratification of the Eighteenth Amendment on January 16, 1919. As early as 1862, preachers representing the Sons of Temperance warned local residents of the dangers of alcohol consumption. It was a warning well advised because San Rafael had always been known as a town with an ample supply of saloons, one at least on every street corner. Newspapers of the Prohibition Era advised their readers that, with a doctor's prescription and for medicinal purposes, two and one-half gallons of beer could be purchased every ten days or two quarts of wine every ten days, but not simultaneously.

San Rafael itself achieved some notoriety in the October 17, 1931, edition of the *San Francisco Examiner* when it was revealed that federal marshals had served abatement notices on 16 city establishments that served alcohol. It seems that when the bootleggers were arrested by the local police, they pleaded guilty and were fined, the standard rate being $125 per conviction. Police Chief Peter O'Brien was quoted as saying, "Yes, that's the way we do business. Every so often we raid the boys, and they pay a fine. The money helps to keep up the police and fire departments and keeps the tax rate down."

———————————

Below: The San Quentin baseball team is shown in this photo taken around 1910. The inmates were required to wear striped uniforms until 1913. Not everyone in this picture appears happy to be photographed. Courtesy, Bancroft Library

Facing page: San Quentin Prison is pictured in this 1900 photo. The panoramic view shows the bastille-like turrets and large enclosed yard. To the left outside the walls are the houses and offices of the warden and prison employees. Despite its ominous presence, the prison has economically benefited Marin County and the City of San Rafael. Courtesy, Bancroft Library

But the more substantial change in the city's community life was, once again, transportation. The automobile had transformed family life and business practice. The Hotel Rafael could no longer count on its guests taking long leisurely stays in its commodious rooms and beautiful gardens, for the automobile encouraged travel and visits to many other scenic places. These sights still attracted visitors from San Francisco and the Bay Area, but there was no easy access to San Rafael and Marin County.

The time had come for a San Francisco ferry devoted exclusively to automobiles rather than passengers. The man with the idea was Harry Speas, who established the Golden Gate Ferry in 1922. It was an instant success and continued in operation until 1929 when the Southern Pacific Railroad, which had un-successfully tried to compete, bought the auto ferry and renamed it the Southern Pacific Golden Gate Ferry.

But even as this business deal was struck, the auto ferry was growing obsolete. Industrial progress in the past fifty years had given suburban Americans the railroad, steam and electric, and now the affordable automobile. The new uses of steel would result in a bridge giving to San Rafael and Marin County a highway in the sky over the churning waters of the Golden Gate. The new bridge would fulfill an old dream and transform San Rafael in ways it could scarcely imagine. If railroads and auto ferries would soon be a thing of the past, the Golden Gate Bridge and the American love affair with the automobile would have a longer future.

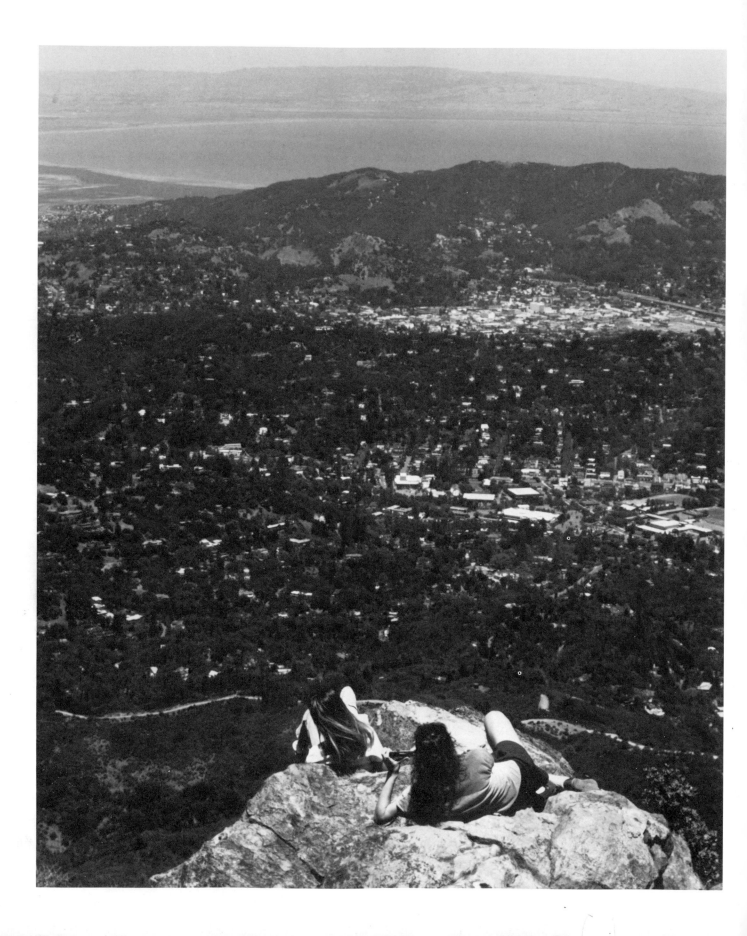

CHAPTER 8

THE METROPOLIS OF MARIN

San Rafael in the 1930s was, with the rest of the nation, in the throes of the Great Depression. Because it was not a city with a large laboring class, it was not as severely affected as some others. Yet economic pressures were real enough, and its relative remoteness seemed designed to keep the small city insulated from the larger urban centers nearby and from any hope for full economic recovery. The population in 1930 was 8,000.

Nevertheless, a series of events was taking shape that its citizens could then have scarcely imagined, events that would give to San Rafael a prominence it has never relinquished. Although in an earlier time the routing of a railroad had placed the city on a short spur line with infrequent service, the modern period would place it squarely at the center of both transportation and economic development in Marin County. All roads would lead to San Rafael.

The initiative for change came first from within. The Marin County Board of Supervisors approached the U.S. Army with a bold plan to purchase a 776-acre tract near present-day Novato and give it to the Army to serve as an air base. With the construction of an airfield, hangars, and buildings, and with many servicemen and women located nearby, there would be a new source of money to pump into a stagnant econ-

omy. The Army agreed and so did the voters who approved a tax increase to purchase the acreage. The land that was then known as "Marin Meadows" later became the Hamilton Air Force Base.

Even with the land donated, the Army had only limited funds for construction. Fortunately, the local initiative coincided with the national election in 1932 that saw the victory of President Franklin D. Roosevelt. To get the country moving again, Roosevelt started a public works program, part of which was devoted to military installations. The Hamilton Field project was able to secure $3,700,000 in federal funds, which enabled the work to get underway and be completed by 1934. By the end of 1933 the payroll at the base was $30,000 monthly, and the servicemen and women were shopping and looking for housing. The base commander turned to the San Rafael Chamber of Commerce for assistance and wrote a letter inquiring whether furnished and unfurnished homes were avail-

Facing page: Looking down on Corte Madera from Mount Tamalpais. Photo by Mark E. Gibson

Above: Girls from San Rafael High School raced across the newly opened Golden Gate Bridge on May 27, 1937. The three seen above are (l-r) Roberta Keaton, Barbara Trondsen, and Evelyn Durant. Courtesy, Dewey Livingston, Inverness Foundation

83

able "in the range of $10 to $25 monthly."

Another major industrial project would have an even greater impact on the City of San Rafael. And though it began in the same decade, this monumental work had been alive in men's imagination for some time. It was the Golden Gate Bridge.

The idea of a bridge spanning the Golden Gate and uniting San Francisco with the northern counties had been around a very long time. In 1868 the *Marin Journal* noted "a company has organized in San Francisco for the purpose of building a bridge from Lime Point in this county to Fort Point in San Francisco. The distance across at the point where it is proposed to build the bridge is one mile."

In the following year, a well-known San Francisco character, Emperor Norton, issued a proclamation:

We Norton, I, Dei Gratia, Emperor of the United States and Protector of Mexico do order and direct that a suspension bridge be constructed at Oakland Point to Yerba Buena Island from thence to the mountain range of Sausalito and from thence to the Farallones. *Whereof fail not under pain of death.*

Joshua (Emperor) Norton was a pleasant lunatic who amused the citizens of San Francisco by his imperial clothes and his sporadic collection of "taxes" from bars, hotels, and businesses whenever he needed a handout. Yet Emperor Norton was speaking with a sense of common yearning, if not reality, in proclaiming that a bridge should be constructed across the Golden Gate.

For a long time the ferries had well served the passengers going from San Francisco to Marin County or the East Bay. They matched the slower pace of travel represented by the horse-drawn carriage and the electric train. The coming of the automobile, however, created problems that the ferries could no longer handle.

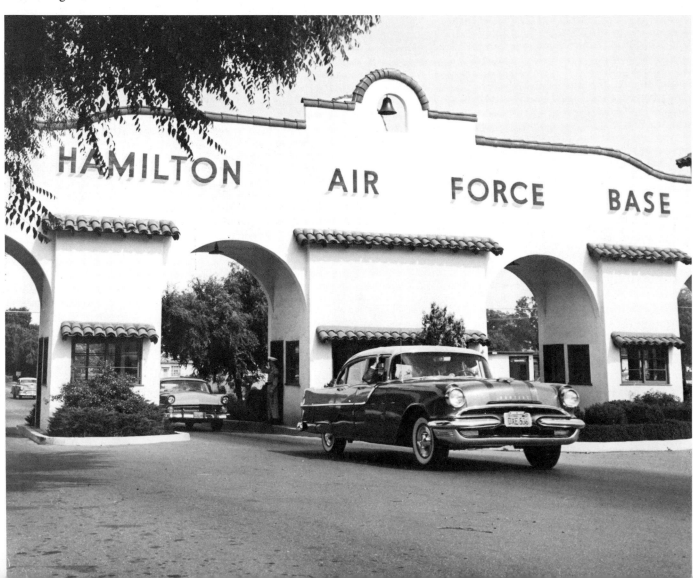

In 1910 in all of California there were but 44,000 automobiles; by 1919 there were 600,000 car owners. In that same year 123,000 autos were ferried across the Golden Gate. Less than ten years later, the number ferried annually was over 2 million. One Labor Day weekend in 1930, San Rafael witnessed the worst traffic jam in its history, with lines of cars bumper to bumper extended north for ten miles. Not even the fourteen ferry boats pressed into service could meet the demand.

It is an interesting twist of history that the one who first aroused the public to the real possibility of the Golden Gate Bridge was a San Rafael man who was the son of the first Marin County commuter. In 1864, James H. Wilkins' father, Hepburn Wilkins, had regularly paid Captain Charles Minter $3 for a round trip from Point San Quentin to San Francisco on the steamer *Petaluma*. Now, in 1916, James Wilkins wrote a series of newspaper articles in the *San Francisco Bulletin* on the feasibility of a bridge across the Golden Gate. He was a well-known figure in northern California, having founded a newspaper, the Marin County *Tocsin* in 1879 when he was only 27 years of age. Later, in 1927, he was elected mayor of San Rafael at age 77.

In his first column, Wilkins noted:

The northern counties are almost an empire in extent, with potentialities barely surface-scratched ... Nature had, in a way, tied their fortunes, beyond recall, to San Francisco. That city must always be their final marketplace—the clearing house.

Wilkins had graduated from the University of California (Berkeley) in civil engineering, and he wrote convincingly about the bridge as he envisioned it. It would

Above, right: The formal portrait of Norton I, "Emperor of the United States and Protector of Mexico," was executed with Norton in full uniform, plumed hat, gilt epaulettes, and curved sword. Joshua A. Norton came to San Francisco in 1849, made and lost a fortune, then became a great success as Emperor Norton I. He died in 1880. Courtesy, Bancroft Library

Facing page: This Spanish-style entrance to Hamilton Air Force Base was very familiar to many thousands of airmen and their families before and after World War II. It remains standing today as a reminder of the vital role the base played in the economic development of San Rafael and Marin County during the early 1930s. Courtesy, Marin Independent Journal

have a suspension span of 3,000 feet and two side spans of 1,000 feet each, be located between Lime Point in Marin and Fort Point in San Francisco, and cost ten million dollars.

That prediction was not so far from reality when the Golden Gate Bridge was completed twenty years later, with a single span of 4,200 feet and two side spans of 1,125 feet each. Indeed, at the time, the Marin County Board of Supervisors was so impressed they invited Wilkins to a special meeting, to be held at the headquarters of the San Rafael Chamber of Commerce in the fall of 1916. San Rafael quickly saw the many advantages of a Golden Gate Bridge, and the San Rafael Chamber of Commerce came out that year for the bridge.

Wilkins' newspaper columns were also read by the San Francisco city engineer M.M. O'Shaughnessy. When World War I was over, O'Shaughnessy contacted several engineers and asked them whether a Golden Gate Bridge could be constructed. One failed to respond. Another estimated the cost at $56 million and so disqualified himself. The one who responded with conviction, a plan, and within budget, was Joseph B. Strauss. The story of the building of the Golden Gate Bridge is usually told in terms of the brief four years, 1933 to 1937, when it was actually constructed. Yet serious effort to study and plan began in 1918 when engineer Strauss submitted his estimates to M.M. O'Shaughnessy. Strauss estimated the cost at $25 million, not far from the actual $35 million it took to complete the bridge.

There were many skeptics. Most did not deny the bridge would be useful but denied it could be built. The waters were too turbulent, and the ocean floor too soft. The railroad and ferry interests, represented by the Southern Pacific, were opposed to the span for they assumed, rightly as things turned out, that the bridge would end the auto ferry. And even if it were constructed, military men worried that enemy bombers might one day destroy it and block the entrance to the strategic port of San Francisco with its wreckage.

A campaign to make Bay Area citizens "bridge-minded" as Joseph Strauss put it, was begun. Frank P. Doyle, a Santa Rosa banker known as the "Father of the Golden Gate Bridge," called a meeting of politicians, businessmen, and bankers in Sonoma County as early as 1923. It was a difficult time in the nation's history for new enterprises. Yet, in the depths of the Depression and with no government funds involved, the Golden Gate Bridge was built. A.P. Giannini of the Bank of America stood ready to fund the project, saying, "San Francisco needs that bridge. We will take the bonds." Wages of $750,000 a year were paid for several years, and the economy of the area was given new life.

But the Golden Gate Bridge has remained something far more than a financial success or a bold engineering innovation. Its contribution to the Bay Area economy during the Depression years is scarcely remembered today. What has remained is the genius of Joseph B. Strauss and the design of Charles Ellis for the remarkably beautiful twin orange towers with a lacing of cables suspended between them holding up a highway in the heavens. The opposition is gone. Now there are only fans and supporters. Fifty years after its construction, motorists still find a thrill in crossing the Golden Gate Bridge. J. Lawrence Toole put it best:

> Its glittering bars are the breakers high,
> Its hinges are hills of granite.
> Its bolts are the winds, its arch the sky,
> Its cornerstone a planet.

Above, left: When Don Timoteo Murphy died in 1852 he bequeathed a school to the Catholic Church. The site and many buildings is known as the St. Vincent's School for Boys, located near Marinwood just south of Novato and Hamilton Field. By 1930 Msgr. Francis P. McElroy had raised funds and completed building the large Italian Renaissance Mission-style church shown in this photo. St. Vincent's School is the oldest institution in California dedicated to the care of boys with special needs. Courtesy, San Rafael Chamber of Commerce.

Facing page: In this 1922 photo members of the San Rafael Chamber of Commerce posed in front of the Rafael Hotel wearing the fashionable straw hats of the period. The Chamber of Commerce has always been a progressive force in the affairs of the city and the county. From its earliest days it has provided a business and professional forum and has initiated services for the betterment of the city and its citizens. Courtesy, San Rafael Chamber of Commerce

On May 27, 1937, the bridge was opened for pedestrians, and the following day it was officially opened for automobiles. And while the ferries remained for a few years, the days of water transport to San Rafael and Marin County were almost over. Now power and sail boats would bring visitors on leisurely cruises across the bay. The commercial auto ferry would be no more, though passenger ferries would take their place. WHERE IS RICHMOND SAN RAFAEL AUTO FERRY?

Whereas in the past one spoke of horses, ferries, and trains, the new word would be "highway." With the opening of the Golden Gate Bridge, traffic to San Rafael and Marin County increased. On the weekends then as now, thousands crossed over from the bustling city to the bucolic haunts and seacoast hamlets of Marin. Traffic to San Rafael was especially heavy, and in 1941 a skyway of five city blocks was opened spanning the San Rafael Creek at Irwin Street. Auto passengers could now view on left and right the trees planted by William Coleman and catch glimpses of the nineteenth-century homes in what was once known as "Coleman's Addition" and is still called "Magnolia" by older residents or "Dominican" by others.

In retrospect it appears that the building of Hamilton Air Field and the Golden Gate Bridge were exercises in prophecy. Few suspected in the 1930s that the United States would soon be embroiled in a world war with battlefronts thousands of miles away across two mighty oceans. Nonetheless, almost in anticipation of World War II, Marin County encouraged the development of an airfield which later became headquarters

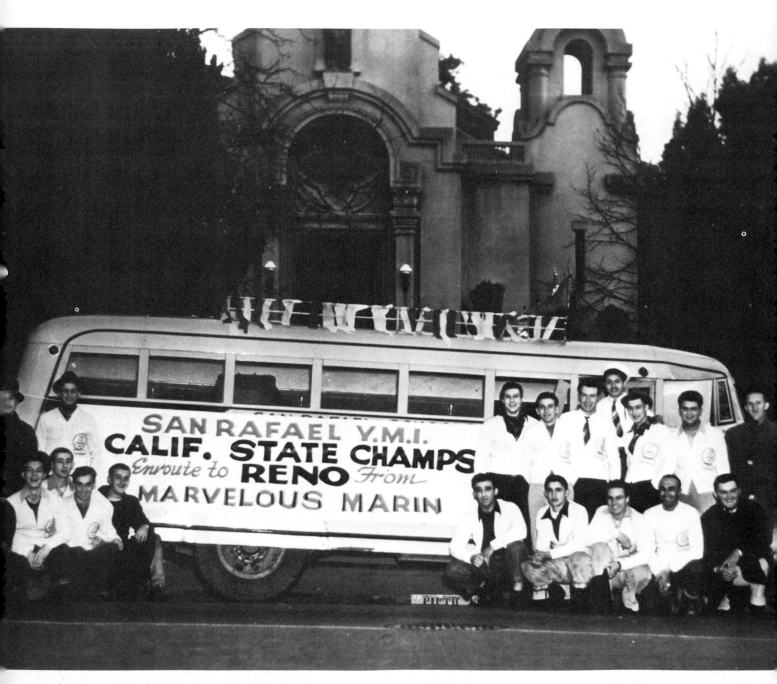

for the Western North American Air Defense Command and a bridge that allowed military transport and maritime supplies to reach Marinship, one of the largest shipbuilding centers on the west coast.

San Rafael's first blackout occurred on December 8, 1941, one day after the Japanese attacked Pearl Harbor in Hawaii. Seventy-five deputy sheriffs were sworn in and began guarding the facilities of the Marin Water District. The possibility of a Japanese invasion was very real. On March 5, 1942, the *Marin Journal* announced there would be a discussion at San Rafael

High School on the subject: "Can Americans take it if an Invasion comes?"

A hostile invasion never came, but an invasion of shipyard workers did. W.H. Bechtel, vice president of Marin Shipbuilding and Bechtel Co., announced in

Above: The San Rafael Y.M.I. basketball team, photographed in 1939. Courtesy, Marin County Historical Society

Left: The Dixie School House. Photo by Mark E. Gibson

Below: The Richmond-San Rafael Bridge connects San Rafael with East Bay areas. Photo by Mark E. Gibson

Above: When the Mission San Rafael was established in 1817, bells such as these were rung to call new Indian converts to work or prayer. Photo by Mark E. Gibson

Left: The statue above the entrance to the Mission San Rafael symbolizes the Spaniards' desire to civilize and bring Christianity to California's native population. Photo by Mark E. Gibson

The Marin County Museum in San Rafael's Boyd Park. Photo by Audrey Gibson

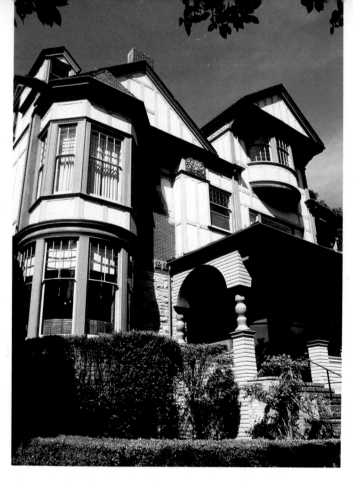

Facing page, top: Falkirk Community Center; the plaque giving a brief history of the building. Photos by Audrey Gibson

Facing page, bottom: The shoreline at China Camp State Park in San Rafael. Photo by George Elich

Above: Mount Tamalpais offers breathtaking views of San Rafael and the Bay area. This vantage point looks south towards Richardson's Bay and San Francisco. Photo by Mark E. Gibson

Right: San Rafael's community of Terra Linda is comfortably nestled among the Marin hills. Photo by Mark E. Gibson

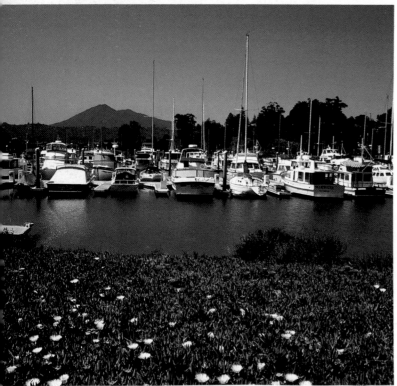

Above: Marin's beautiful Lagunitas Lake. Mount Tamalpais is visible in the distance. Photo by Mark E. Gibson

Left: The marina at San Rafael is home to an assortment of pleasure craft. Mount Tamalpais rises in the distance. Photo by Mark E. Gibson

Facing page: The Muir Woods, near San Rafael, is a beautiful forest of Redwood trees, some nearly 2,000 years old. The Miwok Indians fashioned cone-shaped homes using the bark of these trees. Photo by Mark E. Gibson

Right: The classic lines of the four-story Dominican motherhouse and school built in 1889 are shown here with an overlay of spring blossoms. The land on which it stands was donated by William T. Coleman. This photomontage, entitled "Marin Victorian," is the work of Sister Adele, O.P., Artist-in-Residence, Dominican College.

Below: The shrimp fishing boats along China Camp's shore are depicted here. This unusual view looking northwest out on San Pablo Bay is a photomontage entitled "Respite," done by Sister Adele O.P., Artist-in-Residence, Dominican College

March 1942 that thousands of workers would be employed at the huge shipbuilding yard to be constructed on Richardson's Bay near Sausalito, what we know today as Marin City. Bechtel stated that "the problem for Marin County is to see that these workers have suitable housing accommodations." The earlier requests for housing for the Hamilton Field airmen and women were minor, indeed, compared to the new demands placed upon the homeowners of San Rafael and Marin County in 1942.

The first housing was constructed near the shipyards in the form of 1,200 dormitory rooms for single workers. Then 1,500 family apartments and houses were built nearby. By the end of the first year, the population of Marinship was 5,500. When production hit its peak, 15,000 workers with two hundred specialized skills were working for Marinship. It became one of the first racially integrated housing communities in the country, with 60 percent of the workers white and

Above: Marinship, near today's Marin City, was a major shipbuilding center during World War II. In this war-time photo the famous American contralto Marian Anderson appears before hundreds of construction and clerical workers. In the background are the scaffoldings where the hulls of the Liberty ships and tankers were assembled. Courtesy, Anne T. Kent California Room, Marin County Library

To Bing
from Marinship Boys

40 percent black. Women also made a major contribution as boilermakers, drillers, and sheet-metal workers. Three thousand workers, 20 percent of the work force, were women.

In three and one-half years of production, Marinship saw 93 vessels slide into the waters of Richardson Bay, along with 15 Liberty ships and 78 oil tankers. The plant had an enviable safety record. Not a single ship ever had a major structural or power failure. The first vessel, the *William A. Richardson,* a Liberty ship, was christened on September 26, 1942, and a second, the *William T. Coleman,* a month later. An oil tanker, the *S.S. Mission San Rafael,* was launched on December 31, 1943, after being built in 97 days. By early 1945 Marinship had produced a tanker that required only 33 days from laying the keel to completion, faster than any comparable tanker had ever before been delivered by an American shipyard.

War and the preparation for war were not the only events affecting San Rafael in these difficult years, as commercial enterprise continued to progress. In October 1942, Albert's Department Store opened, and it was described as "the Redwood Empire's Finest." Constructed by Jacob Albert who had come to San Rafael before the turn of the century, the new department store included a third floor assembly room holding 250 people, which was available for social and business groups. In the next year civic leader Jacob Albert celebrated his Golden Anniversary of business in San Rafael.

With the war over in 1945, San Rafael turned again to peaceful pursuits, but the small city had changed. Once again, San Rafael had been discovered. The population of 11,000 in 1945 became almost 14,000 in 1950 and by 1960 had grown to 20,000. By 1970 San Rafael almost doubled its population at 39,000.

The way to San Francisco had been opened by the Golden Gate Bridge, and the postwar years saw the city become accessible also to the East Bay. The old Richmond-San Rafael ferry had been in service since 1915 under the pioneering efforts of Charles Van Damme. During the war, strikes were unknown, but afterwards a series of work stoppages made both Marin County and the City of Richmond impatient. A bridge seemed to be the answer. After three years of construction, a four-mile long bridge was completed in 1956, opening on August 31. The cost of the Richmond-San Rafael Bridge was $68 million, almost twice the cost of the Golden Gate Bridge. It

remains today as the easiest access route to San Rafael and Marin County for East Bay residents. And because it has two levels of traffic for opposing car routes, and an excellent safety record, it has been called the safest highway in California.

With the opening of the Richmond-San Rafael Bridge, the city of San Rafael was now open to traffic from every direction, north and south, east and west. The two bridges had ended forever its isolation and, however remote it may have been in an earlier age, it was now at the very crossroads of northern California.

As Marin's county seat, San Rafael was cast in a leadership role as both the city and county grew during

Facing page: Celebrities such as Bing Crosby came to Marinship during World War II to help keep up the workers' morale. In this 1943 photo, Crosby is being presented with a gift from "The Marinship Boys," and he flashes his famous smile. Courtesy, Anne T. Kent California Room, Marin County Library

Above: San Rafael's Fourth Street was struck by fire between D and E streets on July 30, 1957. Courtesy, Marin County Historical Society

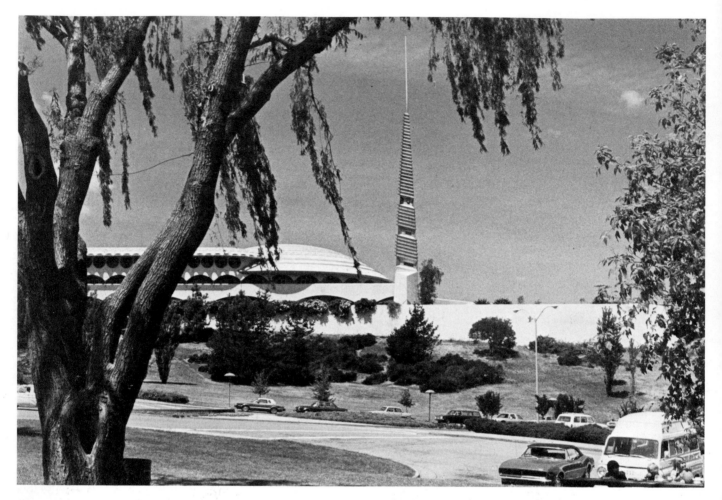

the postwar years. Its new prominence did not, however, move it to abandon its own traditions. The style of gracious living and the natural beauty of the region would be retained in any future planning. Modern California cities are often put to the test of choosing between higher density and loss of living space or a more controlled plan emphasizing the quality of life and respect for nature. San Rafael and Marin County faced this choice in the decision to build a new county courthouse.

Because the old classical courthouse, erected in 1874, was too small, county offices then occupied a dozen other locations throughout the city. It was time for a new courthouse and a new central site. The Board of Supervisors began as early as 1953 to acquire property north of San Rafael in the area known as Santa Venetia.

The civic decision for more open space was accompanied by another decision that indicated clearly enough that the future of the region would be determined by standards of beauty and form as well as

efficiency and economy. The Supervisors selected the eminent Frank Lloyd Wright as principal architect. On July 29, 1957, Wright spoke to the people at the San Rafael High School telling them that "the good building is not one that hurts the landscape but one that makes it more beautiful than before." Later, he added: "In Marin County you have one of the most beautiful landscapes I have ever seen, and I am proud to make the building of the county characteristic of the beauty of the county."

When he was first taken to the site, Wright looked at the small hills rising from the earth and declared, "I'm going to bridge those hills with graceful arches." And he did. Several low springing arches connect the hills and form the base of the two long structures which move in either direction from a central blue core. A 172-foot tower rises alongside the building at the center, while inside a horizontal skylight running the entire length of the building suffuses all the floors below with a natural light. At night it appears to be an ocean liner at sea with its porthole windows aglow.

The design, the site, and the architect were all subject to intense debate during the period of construction of the new Civic Center. Alternatives were suggested, but they did not satisfy the county's need for a single, central site and building. Ground was broken on February 15, 1960, and the first section, the Administration Building, was completed October 13, 1962. The second and larger part, the Hall of Justice, was occupied in December 1969.

The Marin Civic Center was Frank Lloyd Wright's last architectural project. He died in 1959, at the age of 92. It is also the only one of his major designs financed by public funds. Visitors come from around the world to see it. It stands today as both a monument to his ideas and as a statement of Marin County citizens to maintain the harmony between beauty, art, and nature.

As if to give emphasis to the new beginnings represented by the Civic Center, the old courthouse in downtown San Rafael caught fire on May 25, 1971. The interior of the structure was completely gutted. The courthouse was later demolished, making way for a downtown renaissance.

With a new Civic Center, an increased population, and with ready access to San Francisco and the Bay area by the two bridges, San Rafael faced many challenges. As before, it responded with respect for the past and confidence in the future. Eager to maintain its high quality of life, the city moved its boundaries through a series of annexations during the 1950s and 1960s. Areas east of the city toward McNear's Point, including Loch Lomand, Glenwood, and Peacock Gap, were incorporated, as well as large tracts north of the Civic Center, making way for housing and shopping. Terra Linda, part of the old Freitas Ranch, was developed with several thousand houses built, and in 1969 over 1,000 acres, including the Civic Center and adjacent lands, became part of San Rafael. To service the shopping needs of the citizens, especially in the newer portions of the city, the Northgate Mall was opened in the mid-1960s. It is the largest regional shopping center in Marin County.

Today San Rafael is the geographical, financial, and political center of Marin County, while it retains much of the charm of its earlier history. A walk downtown will connect one with the Mission days amid modern banks and progressive stores and delightful restaurants, while a tour of the Civic Center spreads the whole of the new San Rafael at one's feet.

As San Rafael moves into the last decade of the twentieth century, it looks back upon a history that has seen a bountiful land matched by the progress of man. The Civic Center may be taken as a microcosm of the city itself, for as it sits astride the low-lying hills, with its tower pointing to the sky, it represents a society that enhances the natural beauty of the land while providing a splendid human habitation for industrious and progressive people.

San Rafael has learned to balance the pursuit of leisure with the needs of business and commerce. Today it is the only community in Marin with more workers coming into it than out of it. Even for those who work here the attractions are compelling. But whether one works or plays in the Mission City, the same healthful climate and natural beauty that once brought priest and pioneer across the waters of the Bay remain to entice the future visitor.

Above, and facing page: Frank Lloyd Wright, the world-famous architect who designed the Marin County courthouse in San Rafael, is shown in this 1950s photo leaning over one of his drawings. He was the founder of "organic architecture," whereby natural principles dictate form, structure, and detail. Wright was 90 years old when he began his work in Marin County. Courtesy, Anne T. Kent California Room, Marin County Library

CHAPTER 9

PARTNERS IN PROGRESS

Though San Rafael is located only minutes from the business district of San Francisco, the port of Oakland, and major South Bay manufacturing, industrial, and high-technology centers, it is worlds apart from these areas' bustle, congestion, and high prices. In fact, in the early years of this century San Rafael was known primarily as an elite resort town—a "retreat" for wealthy San Franciscans and a tourist haven for travelers from around the world. When the city's main resort hotel, the 200-room Hotel Rafael, burnt to the ground in 1928, San Rafael lost much of its tourist trade—only to regain it in the 1960s and 1970s as the gateway to the Sonoma-Napa wine country and Marin's clean, clear ocean beaches. Today the city's fine restaurants and hotels and picturesque canal area attract not only vacationers but also business travelers who want to be near San Francisco yet relax in a warm country setting.

The new San Rafael resident will find a close-knit community offering excellent public and private schools, comprehensive city services, quality hospitals, and two large convenient shopping areas providing all kinds of goods and services for the city's ethnically diverse population of families, career-minded young people, and senior citizens. The city can boast of no less than three major medical centers, several home-grown banks and financial institutions, and even its own AM-FM radio station.

Historically, San Rafael was incorporated as Marin County's first self-governing municipality. After San Rafael became a full-fledged city in 1910, its voters adopted a city charter, making it the first and only city in Marin County with a charter form of government. This kind of independent thinking has been carried on in modern times by the city's larger corporations, smaller businesses and merchants, chamber of commerce, and city government—all of which try to work

together to maintain San Rafael's high quality of life.

In the 1930s public and private interests were an influential force in supporting the construction of the Golden Gate Bridge and Highway 101. After World War II the chamber of commerce and city government worked together to find housing for the Sausalito shipyard workers and Hamilton Air Field personnel who wanted to relocate permanently in the city. In the 1970s San Rafael's retail merchants got together to pass several downtown redevelopment projects. And in the 1980s some of the city's large corporations have been important factors in introducing new forms of public transportation.

The community has almost always been united on one issue—concern for its natural scenic environment. Land-use zoning ordinances and "open-space" acquisition policies have never permitted San Rafael to become burdened with many common problems of urban blight. Instead, the city has succeeded in attracting several major players in the nonpolluting financial, insurance, and high-technology industries.

As disparate a group as San Rafael's businesses are, they all seem to have one thing in common: a great interest in, and commitment to, their city. The organizations whose histories are related on the following pages have chosen to support this important literary and civic project as another way in which they contribute to the strength of San Rafael.

Facing page: The City of San Rafael enjoyed a Fourth of July parade down Fourth Street in 1885. This era in San Rafael's history was marked by civic progress and social refinement, as citizens such as William T. Coleman and Julia Gilbert provided the impetus to establish schools, provide services, and expand public utilities. Courtesy, Marin County Historical Society

SAN RAFAEL CHAMBER OF COMMERCE

On August 23, 1920, the day the San Rafael Chamber of Commerce was founded, the city was vastly different from the San Rafael of today. The city had a population of 5,500. Fourth Street was lined with venerable old homes, picket fences, small stores, and the imposing Marin Courthouse. Hitching posts and water troughs were still plentiful, and ornate chandelier streetlamps lighted the quiet town at night.

The Chamber was founded by a small group of Fourth Street merchants led by Jake Albert, Siegfried K. Herzog, Sr., George V. Kaenel, and Guy Kirner. In the 1920s the Chamber frequently held social gatherings, such as dinner-dances at the Hotel Rafael—the town's major tourist attraction until 1928, when it was destroyed by fire.

When former Superior Court Judge Carlo R. Freitas suggested that the Chamber incorporate in 1930, the organization officially "got down to business." The incorporation papers stated the Chamber's goals and purposes, most of which still apply: "To build up the city of San Rafael . . . to encourage and assist in public improvements of all kinds . . . to attract and locate schools, colleges, and industrial and manufacturing enterprises . . . to promote commerce, industry, and the physical and moral development of the city."

The Chamber's early business activities reflected the lean Depression

The San Rafael Chamber of Commerce building at 818 Fifth Avenue.

years. In 1932 the Chamber organized its first Trade at Home Festival, designed to boost San Rafael business among the local populace. Later in that troubled decade it supported many projects that would eventually prove indispensable to San Rafael's growth and prosperity, among them the widening of Fourth Street, the building of the Golden Gate Bridge, and the construction of Highway 101.

During World War II San Rafael grew rapidly, serving as a residential and business center for the thousands of people who came to work at the Sausalito shipyards and to serve at Hamilton Air Force Base. The Chamber helped many of these people relocate and settle in San Rafael after the war.

The Chamber was a major factor in stimulating San Rafael's growth and business environment during the 1950s and 1960s. It backed the building of the Richmond-San Rafael Bridge in 1953 and inaugurated the Marin Visitors' Bureau as part of the organization five years later. The Chamber actively participated in the extensive downtown redevelopment project of 1963 and in the beautification program of east San Rafael and the Canal Area in the late 1960s.

Today, with nearly 800 members, the San Rafael Chamber of Commerce is more active than ever. Committees work constantly to bring visitors, tourists, and new business and industry to San Rafael. Daily the Chamber office at 818 Fifth Avenue sends out information packets about the city, fields numerous phone calls from prospective visitors about local attractions and facilities, and maintains up-to-date information files on a wide range of local statistics and activities.

The organization also offers its members a voice in legislation by monitoring national, state, county, and local bills that affect the San Rafael business community, then surveying members on important issues and presenting the survey results to lawmakers. A representative of the group attends every city council meeting and, when appropriate, makes presentations on behalf of the business community. Recent projects include working with county and city officials on solutions to the city's transportation and traffic problems, coordinating a crime prevention program with the San Rafael police department, and endorsing a Senior Citizen Gold Card Program to benefit senior citizens and local merchants.

Members receive a wide variety of useful services and publications, including the monthly *Chamberaction* newsletter and the annual *San Rafael Business Directory,* which is mailed to all San Rafael households. In addition, the Chamber regularly offers seminars and workshops to keep members up to date on the newest business techniques, new comprehensive health plan coverage, and a customer/client referral service.

Chamber-sponsored events, such as the annual Parade of Lights opening the holiday season, the Candidate's Forum (cosponsored with the League of Women Voters), and the annual State of the City Dinner are well known throughout the community.

As it has been for more than a half-century, the San Rafael Chamber of Commerce will be the city's central unifying force, working with merchants, industry, schools, police and fire departments, redevelopment commission, and city government, making San Rafael a better place to live and work.

NEW HORIZONS SAVINGS AND LOAN ASSOCIATION

New Horizons Savings and Loan Association originated with—and is currently directed and managed by—members of the local business community. Since its first day of operation in 1980, the Association has grown steadily, and this excellent growth record has earned New Horizons a four-star, high-performance rating in the savings and loan industry, based on return on equity and net worth.

New Horizons was organized as a Marin-based savings and loan association, to be supported by sound investments mostly in Marin County. The Association has achieved its excellent performance by maintaining this focus.

Today New Horizons Savings and Loan Association has over $100 million in total assets and services more than 6,500 savings accounts. In its six years of operation the Association has made more than 1,000 real estate loans to Marin County families and has been entrusted with over $90 million in savings deposits. Currently approximately 560 shareholders own a total of 719,436 shares of New Horizons stock.

The Association's success may be attributed to several factors. First, New Horizons has had strong, stable leadership since its inception. James W. Barnett, president and chairman of the board, is a longtime Marin County resident with 30 years of experience in the savings and loan business. Other members of the board—all original directors—include Jody Anne Becker, program coordinator for Marin County Mediation Services; C. Paul Bettini, former San Rafael mayor and currently an insurance broker and agent; JoAnne Fabian, San Rafael attorney; Pat Glasner, Corte Madera realtor; Howard P. Hetzner, retired Standard Oil Company executive; R. Douglas Norby, president of Lucasfilm Ltd.; Iris C. Pera, owner of a San Rafael financial analysis firm; George J. Silvestri, Jr., San Rafael attorney; and Judith A. Waller of Greenbrae, owner of an engineering consulting firm.

Second, sound operating strategies and prudent management have been instrumental in New Horizons' success. The Association caters to depositors who seek higher interest rates and specializes in short-term and variable-rate real estate loans. New Horizons invests about 75 percent of its funds in Marin County, concentrating on custom home construction, but also acting as a custom lender to individuals and organizations.

Finally, civic involvement has been a key factor in New Horizons' acceptance by, and growth in, the community. The Association takes seriously its commitment to San Rafael and Marin County. Over the years New Horizons has sponsored or participated in numerous community projects for such groups as the Chamber of Commerce,

New Horizons Savings and Loan Association is located in Courthouse Square, at 1050 Fourth Street in San Rafael, the heart of Marin County's financial center.

the Marin Symphony Youth Orchestra, the Boy Scouts of America, and the Marin Wildlife Center.

When New Horizons Savings and Loan Association first opened its doors, the founders and Association management believed that a small, service-oriented financial institution would prosper in San Rafael. They were right. New Horizons has met its objective of providing a profitable long-term investment for stockholders in a community-based and community-oriented financial institution and will continue to grow and contribute to the community in the coming years.

GHILOTTI BROS., INC.

When James Ghilotti settled in San Rafael, he had no idea his stonemasonry business would someday evolve into one of Northern California's largest engineering contracting firms. The year was 1914, and Ghilotti had immigrated from the small town of Grozio in northern Italy with his wife, Amalia, and one-year-old son, Willie. Five years earlier he had worked on the damage caused by the San Francisco Earthquake, and now he was in the community to stay.

In those days stonemasonry was a difficult craft but much in demand, and Ghilotti was able to carve out a decent, hard-earned living in the San Rafael area. People in Marin heard about his reputation for high-quality workmanship and for his simple motto: "If I do something wrong, I do it over." By 1918 he had saved enough money to buy one of the first dump trucks in the county, an extravagant, hotly debated family purchase at the time, but one that would later prove instrumental in the family's entrance into cement work—and eventually into one of the firm's major specialties, road and highway paving. He would drive the truck to one of many Marin creeks, shovel gravel from the creekbed into the back of the truck, and haul it to the work site, where he would mix the cement by hand.

Over the next 20 years the Ghilottis' four sons—Willie, Dino, Henry "Babe," and Mario—all participated actively in the family business. As a reward for their work, the business name was changed from James Ghilotti to James Ghilotti and Sons in 1939.

When the United States entered World War II, all four sons joined the service. They returned to find their father involved in many small sidewalk paving jobs. (Many sidewalks in San Rafael still carry the "James Ghilotti" signature.) In the postwar period the brothers learned the construction business from their father and from college engineering courses; as their experi-

James Ghilotti (at center, wearing a suit coat) with his stonemasonry and cement contracting business in 1936. This was the complete company back then and the forerunner of today's Ghilotti Bros., Inc.

ence and knowledge expanded, so did the business—the company's services were now extending to bridge and highway construction.

By 1950, after 36 years in America, the founder was ready to retire and sell the business to his sons. "If I *give* you the business," he told them, "you won't appreciate how much work it takes to succeed. If I sell it to you, you'll realize you have to work to pay for it."

Unfortunately, James Ghilotti was not able to enjoy his hard-earned leisure time; he died only a few months after retiring. The organization changed its name again, this time to Ghilotti Bros., Inc., and moved to new offices at 629 Francisco Boulevard. The "boys" were on their own.

Their father would not have been disappointed by the results: In the past 37 years Ghilotti Bros., Inc., has handled virtually every kind of heavy-construction project, including public highway and bridge construction; site preparation for commercial, industrial, and residential properties; installation of underground systems; hazardous waste cleanup operations; and shoreline protection endeavors.

The firm's varied work can be seen throughout the Bay Area. Ghilotti Bros., Inc., reconstructed the apron at San Francisco Airport and conducted the site preparation for the Village Shopping Mall in Corte Madera, the 250-acre Napa Corporate Park, and the Village in the Park condominium project in Daly City. The grading and underground systems for Hewlett-Packard's industrial complex in Rohnert Park were other accomplishments. Before the exclusive Point Tiburon condominiums were constructed, Ghilotti Bros., Inc., removed 30,000 cubic yards of contaminated dirt and replaced it with 50,000 cubic yards of "clean" dirt—in the midst of heavy seasonal rains.

The corporation has participated in numerous road and highway paving projects. San Rafael's Fourth Street has been repaved twice by Ghilotti Bros., Inc., over the years, and the firm has widened and repaved many stretches of Highway 101 in Marin and on the Peninsula. The entire eight-mile

San Pedro Road was constructed by the company, a project that required sophisticated concrete retaining walls and involved hundreds of curves; it was completed in 1985 after a 20-year period.

In 1950 the organization's annual revenues were $220,000; in 1986 the figure was $35 million. The growth and success of Ghilotti Bros., Inc., may be attributed to many factors, not the least of which is its belief in hiring—and keeping—the best administrative, construction, and engineering personnel. The firm's employee base of 350 people includes many devoted staff members who have been a part of the Ghilotti family for 20 or even 30 years. Some long-termers have children employed by the company.

Capital reinvestment is another factor. In 1950 the operation had an equipment inventory of one bulldozer, a loader, and a couple of dump trucks. Today its fleet of heavy-construction and support equipment, totaling more than 400 pieces, is the largest and most modern machinery in Northern California. Ghilotti Bros., Inc., is one of the few construction firms in the Bay Area with the equipment and skills necessary for night work and for site preparation in all types of ground conditions, from rock to mud to hazardous waste areas.

James Ghilotti's business philosophy—respect for a job well done, and love for the community in which one works and plays—has been continued by the enterprise he founded. The firm's activities in the San Rafael community are almost legendary: the Main Terrace School, YMCA Fund, San Geronimo Valley Community Church, Marin General Hospital, Hanna Boys Center, Marin Civic Ballet Association, St. Rita's Church, St. Raphael's Church, Marin County Day School, and the Jewish Hospital Foundation

A major Bay Area project by Ghilotti Bros., Inc., was the reconstruction of the apron at San Francisco Airport.

are just a few of the many community organizations that have benefited from the company's time, services, and donations.

Since 1962 its headquarters has been located at 525 Jacoby Street, but the corporation also has satellite offices in Santa Rosa, San Francisco, and Richmond—and plans to open another in Vallejo in the near future. In addition, company quarries in Lakeville and Novato enable Ghilotti Bros., Inc., to maintain a stockpile of rock and soil materials.

Of the four brothers originally involved with the operation, Willie died in 1967; Henry founded his own underground systems venture in 1962; Dino is still active as chairman of the board; and Mario is president and chief executive officer. Not surprisingly, the third generation of the Ghilotti family has

Ghilotti Bros., Inc., does a diverse range of heavy construction projects, from public highway, and bridge construction, and site preparation for residential, commercial, and industrial properties, to shoreline protection endeavors.

entered the business: Dino's son Dick is operations manager, and Mario's son Michael has just begun full-time employment with the firm.

In spite of multimillion-dollar construction projects, the company still finds time for occasional residential jobs. "Every now and then," says Mario Ghilotti, "I'll get a call from someone in San Rafael who says 'Your father did a good job for my grandfather, so I know you'll do a good job for me.'"

A reputation like that portends a bright future for Ghilotti Bros., Inc., and for the city of San Rafael.

SHAMROCK MATERIALS

The postwar building boom had a significant effect on the Marin building trades. As Terra Linda, San Marin, and other subdivisions were developed in the late 1940s and early 1950s, the area's contractors kept constantly busy. Local materials suppliers also had their hands full trying to keep up with the contractors' demands for concrete, which they needed to build the new residential and commercial developments popping up all over Marin County.

One such building contractor was Lee R. Ceccotti, a general concrete contractor in Marin and San Francisco, whose raw material needs were just not being met quickly enough. He could have continued to push his suppliers for better service but instead decided to go one step further—he became his own supplier.

So it happened that in June 1954 Ceccotti acquired a controlling interest in Shamrock Materials, the third ready-mix concrete firm in Marin. He began that year with 12 employees and 10 converted Army trucks. Today Shamrock is one of the largest ready-mix concrete suppliers in Northern California, with more than 200 employees and a fleet of 85 modern heavy-load trucks for hauling the material to construction sites in five counties, from the Golden Gate to Ukiah.

Over the years Shamrock has provided ready-mix concrete for literally hundreds of residential buildings, office buildings, parking structures, schools, hospitals, churches, water treatment plants, dams, and bridges throughout Marin, Sonoma, and Napa counties. A few of the many Shamrock projects include Marin County Civic Center Administration Building, Marin General Hospital, Fireman's Fund Phase I, Angel Island Park buildings, McGraw-Hill's book warehouse, and Terra Linda High School, in Marin; Plaza Shopping Center, Sonoma Valley Water Treatment Plant, Stephen Zellerbach Winery, Apple Creek Apartments, Hewlett-Packard, and Kaiser Medical Center, in Sonoma County; and Atrium Retirement Center, Napa Downtown Redevelopment Center, Silverado Winery, and Bedford Industrial Park, in Napa.

Shamrock supplies not only ready-mix concrete but also a wide range of other high-quality building materials, an inventory the company acquired when it purchased Marin Masonry in 1976. Today Shamrock is the largest wholesale and retail supplier of general building materials in the North Bay, offering a full spectrum of blocks, bricks, crushed rock, drain pipe, fireplaces, wood stoves, gravel, plaster, sand, tools, and many other products for residential and commercial construction.

Although the corporation has grown steadily since its founding, its most dramatic growth has occurred since 1980. In 1981 Shamrock acquired ready-mix operations in Santa Rosa, Cotati, and Healdsburg; the following year it acquired companies in Napa, Vallejo, Cloverdale, and Ukiah. The firm currently has 11 branch locations in addition to its headquarters plant at 665 Irwin Street in San Rafael.

Some of the company's recent growth must be attributed to Lee Ceccotti's son, Gene Ceccotti, who joined the operation in 1978. A former business attorney, Gene came on board when one of Shamrock's longtime crucial officers, Lou Delle Valle, passed away unexpectedly. The younger Ceccotti, now chief executive officer, and Max Cerini, president and chief operations officer, have taken the organization in exciting new directions. Cerini was manager of the Novato

plant when it was acquired in 1964, and he now supervises all field operations for Shamrock. A computer software system developed under Ceccotti's tutelage is now marketed nationwide to ready-mix and building materials firms. The data-processing, business management program has already been installed in six major corporate offices, and many more are expected to follow suit in the next few years.

Shamrock has also become a recognized leader in advocating legislation for the construction trades. For example, it was instrumental in passing state legislation in 1986 that enhances the protection of materials suppliers to government jobs.

Considering that the corporation was founded on the need for quick, efficient service, it comes as no surprise that it has been a pioneer in several as-

pects of ready-mix trucking and automated concrete batching operations. As early as 1965 Shamrock started its own trucking company, Cloverleaf Trucking, for hauling its own cement. The organization was also one of the first ready-mix operations to use computerized batch systems for quality control, and computerized truck tracking through two-way radios to assure that effective communication is maintained between the job site and office facilities.

Shamrock's greatest contribution to industry may yet come in the field of materials science. One of only a handful of building materials firms to have a complete quality-control department, Shamrock monitors, and enhances, the quality of its concrete to protect against weather, cracking, and other damage. In addition, the

company's quality-control manager, Ted van Midde, conducts seminars at colleges and universities across the country, educating architects and civil engineers on the latest technological advances in concrete.

Shamrock is also a leader in the community. Through the years the corporation has contributed time, effort, and materials to many civic and charitable organizations such as the YMCA and Albert's Field. As an industry and community leader for 33 years, Shamrock Materials has been, and will continue to be, a major contributor to the economic and physical growth of San Rafael.

One of Shamrock's ready-mix trucks sported a festive look for America's bicentennial in 1976.

DEMING'S MARIN TIRE AND BRAKE
CARLO'S TRANSMISSION SERVICE

Deming's Marin Tire and Brake (above), at 668 Irwin, and Carlo's Transmission Service (inset), just south, have inspired loyalty from their Marin County patrons with their reputation for knowledgeable mechanics and superior service.

For most people, opportunity only knocks but once. In the case of Scott Deming, opportunity knocked twice, and he was able to make the most of it on both occasions. Deming was only 23 years old and working for a transmission rebuilding outfit in San Francisco when Carlo's Transmission Service went up for sale in 1965. Carlo's had a good record and reputation, and Deming had experience and a burning desire to own his own business: He took a second mortgage on his house and purchased the company.

Three years later, with Carlo's running as smoothly as the cars leaving the shop, Deming heard another knock—or, more closely, the sound of fire engine sirens. Only a half-block away on Irwin Street, the San Rafael Tire and Brake building was destroyed by fire. When the owners of the business decided not to rebuild, Deming arranged with the landlord to design the new facility himself and lease it after construction. Deming's Marin Tire and Brake opened in 1970.

Since that time both operations have grown steadily and substantially. In 1970 Carlo's and Marin Tire had eight employees and combined revenues of $80,000. Today Deming manages 30 people and a volume of $2.6 million.

The success of both businesses may be attributed to several factors. The primary reason is a belief in high-quality customer service. "When customers ask why we work so hard to please them," says Deming, "I tell them 'selfishness'—we'll do the best we can for them because we want their business in the future." The result has been a large, dedicated clientele that has been coming to both shops for years. Many customers have their cars serviced with Deming even after moving away from Marin County because

they just won't trust their cars to anyone else.

Employees of both businesses are treated with the same kind of respect, resulting in the same kind of loyalty. The companies' strict promote-from-within policy is inherited directly from the founder's own beginnings: He wants to provide the same opportunity he was afforded almost 20 years ago. Thus, many of Carlo's and Marin Tire's personnel have been with the firms for more than 10 years.

Deming's active participation in San Rafael's community affairs has been another major reason for his firms' success. He currently sits on the boards of seven community and charitable organizations, including the Salvation Army, YMCA, Rotary Club, Exodus (an organization that helps autistic children), and the San Rafael Chamber of Commerce.

Today Carlo's Transmission Service, located in a 5,000-square-foot facility on Irwin Street, maintains its longtime reputation as having the most knowledgeable mechanics in Northern California. Under the expert guidance of master mechanic Bob Haluska, Carlo's uses the latest technology for servicing, repairing, and replacing transmissions for domestic and foreign automobiles and light trucks.

Deming's Marin Tire and Brake, just north of Carlo's at 668 Irwin, is the largest retail tire store in Marin County. It has the only on-the-car balancing system in Marin and is directed by general manager David Steacy; the office is ably run by office manager Gretchen Rehs.

As San Rafael and Marin continue to grow in the years ahead, the outlook for both Carlo's Transmission Service and Deming's Marin Tire and Brake appear bright. If opportunity knocks again, one San Rafael businessman will know how to open the door and offer generous hospitality—good news for both automobile owners and the city of San Rafael.

EARL FARNSWORTH EXPRESS

Earl Farnsworth thought he had a better way. The year was 1971 and Farnsworth was operations manager at Crockett's-Mayflower, an old San Rafael moving firm with some internal problems. Earl had his own ideas about how to run a moving company; after all, he was a third-generation California mover and had been in the business since age 14.

So Earl and his wife, Lenore, decided to take the big step and go it alone. Looking back now, it seems that the Farnsworths made the right decision: While Crockett's dropped entirely off the map, the Earl Farnsworth Express is still rolling along as Marin's leading local and worldwide moving company.

The Farnsworth name goes back many years in the Bay Area moving business—all the way back to the great San Francisco Earthquake, when Earl's grandfather and great-uncle hauled barrels of drinking water to quake victims by horse and wagon. Soon afterwards Farnsworth & Ruggles was founded, and for many years was one of the largest drayage firms on the West Coast.

Earl Farnsworth started in the moving business in 1950, working part time for his stepfather, Dick Hardin, and Hardin's partner, Charles Pierce, who were Bekins agents in San Rafael. He worked for Pierce-Hardin through high school and college and, after a three-year hitch in the Navy, rejoined the firm, then agents for North American, in 1960, as assistant manager. He left to take the Crockett's position in 1968, and the rest, as they say, is history.

Unlike many new companies, Earl Farnsworth Express was successful right from the start. Operating out of their San Rafael home, Earl and Lenore began with only one van and a pickup truck, but within a very short time acquired a great deal of business moving pianos and medium-size households and offices. During these early years the Express delivered new pianos for Steinway, Sherman & Clay, Miracle Music, Dominican College, and a number of piano tuners in the San Rafael area.

With a philosophy of "take care of the customer and they'll use you again," the company grew steadily through the 1970s and early 1980s, moving thousands of households and organizations, such as Pacific Gas & Electric, WestAmerica Bank, Equitable Life Assurance, and Logo Paris. In 1971 Earl and a handful of part-time helpers grossed $60,000; in 1986 the firm had 12 full-time employees and one million dollars in business.

By 1981 Earl Farnsworth was able to construct an ultramodern 40,000-square-foot moving and storage facility, located at 2111 Francisco Boulevard. The facility houses 12,000 square feet of clean, containerized storage space and a climatic-controlled storage vault. The company's new fleet of custom-built air-ride vans includes the latest safety features for moving furniture, computers, and office equipment—even automobiles—damage-free. And as the Marin agent for Mayflower Transit, Farnsworth offers the

Earl Farnsworth Express, with a modern, 40,000-square-foot moving and storage facility and a new fleet of custom-built air-ride vans, is Marin's leading local and worldwide moving company.

efficiency and experience of one of the country's oldest and largest nationwide van lines.

The fourth generation of Farnsworths grew up in the business. Earl Jr. is now assistant manager of the company, and the Farnsworths' younger son, John, started in the sales department in 1986.

Over the past decade Farnsworth Express has been a "mover" in San Rafael civic affairs. The firm donates thousands of boxes for food and toys to the city's needy every Christmas and provides moving services free of charge to the United Way, YMCA, and several other charitable organizations in the San Rafael area.

Sixteen years later the city continues to reap the benefits of Earl Farnsworth's difficult decision. With companies like Earl Farnsworth Express, the city will keep moving in the right direction for many years to come.

Earl Farnsworth follows a family tradition of moving services dating back to the great San Francisco Earthquake, when his grandfather and great-uncle hauled barrels of drinking water to quake victims by horse and wagon. Today Farnsworth Express is the Marin agent for Mayflower Transit.

COLE FINANCIAL GROUP, INC.

San Rafael Mayor Larry Mulryan and Kit Cole cut the ribbon at the opening celebration of the Cole Financial Building.

Over the past two decades women have become much more savvy about the world of finance and have gained considerable influence in business and industry. One of the leaders in these efforts is Kit M. Cole, who has founded several organizations, such as Cole Financial Group, Inc., to improve the position of women in the business, professional, and investment communities of Marin County.

Cole's first major accomplishment was founding the Wednesday Morning Dialogue in 1974. The Dialogue is a group of Marin professional women who meet regularly to make important business contacts and to discuss common career interests. Today the organization boasts a membership of 100 of Marin County's most talented and active female business and civic leaders.

In 1978, as its first chairman of the board, Cole spearheaded a group consisting of 20 Marin women without extensive business experience and three men in forming a new female-owned and -oriented savings and loan association—New Horizons Savings and Loan Association. Beginning with a $2-million investment, the San Rafael association has grown to more than $100 million in assets, and the original stock has increased in value more than 600 percent. New Horizons has expanded its customer base and today serves the needs of the entire Marin County community.

Perhaps Cole's greatest achievement was establishing her own investment advisory and financial planning firm, Cole Financial Group, in 1977. The goal of the company is to provide investment and financial advisory services, with a special focus on the needs of women. "When it comes to investments and financial planning," says Cole, "many women are at a disadvantage. Most traditional school systems have not taught women how to handle money. We are helping to change that."

Cole Financial Group, Inc., offers investment management, financial counseling, and personal money management workshops. Clients can arrange hourly financial counseling to obtain answers to their personal financial questions or receive a complete written personal financial plan that includes detailed recommendations for achieving investment and life-style goals.

While many investment advisors develop a recommended portfolio based on present income, which often means clients must reduce the quality of their life-styles, Cole works with clients to determine their life-style goals and then organizes and manages their portfolios to achieve and support these goals.

With its wide range of investment and family financial services, the firm allows clients free time to spend on other important interests and projects. At the same time clients can be assured that their investments are being monitored on a daily basis and that decisions to improve their portfolios are being made when they should be made.

When engaged as an investment advisor, the firm's expert staff reviews existing securities, recommends sales

and purchases, and arranges the necessary transactions. Cole Financial Group currently manages more than $42 million in stocks, bonds, cash, and real estate for a client base that now extends from Marin County to New York and Europe.

Cole Financial Group also uses its planning skills to accomplish community objectives. Cole co-chaired the Institutional Group, which was the most successful division of the Marin County United Way campaign in 1985, raising almost 50 percent of the total funds contributed in Marin that year.

In addition, the company organizes community leaders to develop more effective means of communication. In 1984 Cole became the co-founder and first president of Marin Forum, a local breakfast group of some 50 Marin County business and civic leaders. Marin Forum meets once a month to provide members the opportunity to become better acquainted and to explore ways of attaining community objectives through combined efforts.

In an advisory capacity Cole has served as a member of the board of directors of the Mill Valley Film Festival and the San Francisco Bay Girl Scout Council. She has taught personal finance at Dominican College and regularly presents personal money management workshops for women in the community.

In October 1985 Cole formed a group to acquire one of Marin County's finest office properties, The Cole Financial Building, at 851 Irwin Street in San Rafael. The property is developing into a major financial center and has attracted other substantial financial institutions of the central San Ra-

The opening of New Horizons Savings and Loan Association, a savings and loan started by Cole and 20 other women with financial emphasis on the needs of women. Today it has more than $100 million in assets and serves the entire Marin County community.

fael area.

Celebrating its 10th anniversary in 1987, Cole Financial Group, Inc., has succeeded in combining its female-oriented business philosophy with its strong belief in, and commitment to, the city of San Rafael. "It's impossible for a community to thrive over a long period of time," states Kit Cole, "if

The Cole Financial Building at 851 Irwin Street—a major financial center in San Rafael.

one-half of its members are not financially secure. By helping women gain control over their financial destinies, we hope to make San Rafael a more prosperous community."

FIREMAN'S FUND

San Francisco burned down five times between 1849 and 1851, the victim of casual architecture, prevailing winds, and high spirits. Eastern insurance companies of the day viewed the city as a carelessly built, Gold Rush backwater town filled with a transient and irresponsible populace. Some of the more venturesome foreign underwriters found that cautious coverage could turn a modest profit, but for the most part they still perceived San Francisco as a primitive outpost.

Even by 1863 insurance protection for serious construction was hard to find, and community leaders despaired in their efforts to attract new capital and build an enduring city on the shores of the bay. Fire fighting was left to volunteer organizations, whose members banded together because of political conviction or place of origin. Fierce rivalries between these groups often worked to the advantage of the blaze, with one ambushing another in order to be the first to arrive at the fire.

During this time an enterprising sea captain named William Holdredge conceived the idea of founding a home-town fire insurance company. He pro-

This Fireman's Fund home office, completed in 1867 in San Francisco, was considered one of the city's most elegant. Chimneys along the roof's edge were connected with a number of coal-burning fireplaces located throughout the building.

posed that the new firm should donate 10 percent of its annual profits to the benefit fund of volunteer firemen, thereby encouraging their diligence in quenching flames erupting from company-insured buildings. The city's merchants and businessmen recognized in Holdredge's proposal a solution to their insurance problems and the possibility of making a profit in the bargain. They eagerly pledged their support.

Incorporated as Fireman's Fund Insurance Company, the firm opened its doors May 6, 1863, with two employees behind the counter, the redoubtable captain at the helm, and some of the most prominent names in California on the board of directors. The fledgling enterprise was a resounding success from the start.

For sound reasons, the arrangement with the firemen was soon terminated by a lump-sum payment of $5,000 in gold coins. Yet, throughout more than a century of significant changes, the colorful name has endured, a respected part of California history.

In 1867 fire insurance companies were granted permission to sell ocean marine insurance. Fireman's Fund, with less than four years of experience under its belt, was cocky enough to plunge right in. Sitting at the edge of one of the world's busiest and fastest growing natural harbors, the company soon gained its sea legs and was writing a significant amount of insurance for ships and their cargoes from around the world.

Fireman's Fund again showed its adventurous spirit when it went against the tide of expansion, moving from west to east as it appointed new agencies and representatives. So successful was this effort that the firm was a well-established underwriter in Chicago in 1873, when that city was destroyed by one of history's most devastating conflagrations. The young organization's losses far exceeded its assets; nonetheless, its president immediately traveled to the scene and pledged full payment. When San Francisco shareholders agreed to pay a special assessment, every valid claim was honored—

For many years Fireman's Fund insured the boats that took bar pilots out to meet ships coming into San Francisco Bay. One of them was the Gracie S., shown at left, with the lightship San Francisco and an incoming freighter.

thereby sparking a flood of national publicity and a spate of new agents eager to sell the policies of a company with such dramatic proof of reliability.

From then on the firm grew steadily and profitably, under the direction of some of the outstanding leaders in western business. Fireman's Fund pioneered new coverages for California's burgeoning agricultural community, fashioned innovative policies to handle the special needs of Alaskan fishing fleets and the imperiled oil-seeking whalers of New England, covered heavy gold shipments from the Yukon, and issued policies on the railroads probing westward.

By the early 1900s Fireman's Fund was an acknowledged leader and innovator in the industry. It had absorbed many smaller western insurers and was experimenting daringly with insurance for motorcars—even if they traveled out of state. The company was a respected force in its always-bustling home city and a creative underwriter of national note.

A few minutes after 5 a.m. on April 18, 1906, San Francisco was jolted awake by a great wrenching of the earth. Buildings throughout the city tilted or collapsed, and gas and water lines ruptured. Even as people tumbled from their beds in the first horrifying moments of the earthquake, fire began to prowl unchecked through the heart of the city. Firemen, powerless without water, could not halt the flames.

Fireman's Fund was ruined, physically and financially. The head office was a charred skeleton. All of its records had perished. The firm's total liability took days to determine, the accounting impeded by the dark knowledge that no insurance company had ever survived such a calamity in its home city.

Yet Fireman's Fund survived—because its shareholders, policyholders, employees, and the citizens of San Francisco willed the resurrection of the

city and its institutions. Survival meant months of frustrating negotiation and compromise; it also meant faith enough on the part of claimants to accept their payment half in cash and half in the stock of the almost-defunct company.

Since 1906 the organization has never been seriously threatened by another catastrophe. It has moved forward—entering new markets, developing new coverages, and acquiring other carriers to broaden its underwriting scope and strengthen its servicing facilities.

Fireman's Fund established a permanent link with Marin County when it provided insurance for the construction of the Golden Gate Bridge. Later the company became a full-time resident—and the county's largest private employer—when it moved its computer operations to San Rafael in 1975 and

Fireman's Fund established its first permanent link to Marin County when it insured construction of the Golden Gate Bridge in the 1930s. The company also provided the performance bond on the contractor who resurfaced the bridge deck almost 50 years later.

its national headquarters to Novato in 1982.

Fireman's Fund is now the nation's 11th-largest property-liability insurer and the fourth-largest insurer of business and industry. The company is equally comfortable protecting the highly technical risk, the small business on Main Street, homes in fine neighborhoods, educational and cultural institutions, entertainment industry endeavors throughout the world, thousands of workers, and millions of vehicles—including some that have ventured into space.

THE MALL AT NORTHGATE

The geographic and demographic core of Northern California's affluent Marin County is the Mission City of San Rafael. At its northern edge, framed by handsome residential neighborhoods and the bustling Northgate commercial area, stands Marin's largest regional shopping center—The Mall at Northgate. Three diverse department stores and more than 100 specialty shops provide a broad spectrum of merchandise and services for the community.

Since its grand opening in 1965, The Mall at Northgate has been a favorite gathering place and fashion mecca for shoppers throughout the north counties of the San Francisco Bay Area. Originally anchored by Emporium-Capwell, the center added a new Sears department store seven years later.

Keeping pace with the economic and population growth of Marin County throughout the 1970s and 1980s, The Mall at Northgate continued to expand, adding many new buildings as well as a third department store, Mervyn's, which opened its doors in 1985.

In 1986, under the ownership of The MaceRich Company and The Northwestern Mutual Life Insurance Company, The Mall at Northgate underwent a major multimillion-dollar enclosure and renovation. The gracious outdoor center was transformed into a dramatic galleria, becoming Marin County's first enclosed mall. Decorative columns rise up to a soaring ceiling boasting skylights and mirrored vaults. Grand archways and theatrical-style lighting emphasize the wide indoor "boulevards." Unique architecture—highlighted by garden areas, sculpture settings, and wood parquet floors—creates a striking combination of maturity and youthful vitality.

Throughout the expansion and architectural improvements over the years, The Mall at Northgate steadfastly maintained its theme of commu-

nity friendship. The mall has always played an active role in community services, hosting Easter Seal benefit auctions, the annual Grape Festivals (benefiting Sunny Hills Children's Services), Humane Society benefits, blood bank drives, annual health fairs, Junior Achievement fairs, KQED (PBS) membership drives, muscular dystrophy fund raisers—the list is endless. The enclosure of The Mall at Northgate further enhanced its ability

The newly renovated Northgate Mall is the shopping hub of Marin County. Photography by Stuart Lirette

to serve community organizations.

The dynamic partnership of The MaceRich Company and Northwestern has brought a new energy to Northgate. Their long-range commitment will continue to position The Mall at Northgate as a good neighbor and cornerstone of the community.

PHOENIX AMERICAN INCORPORATED

When Phoenix Leasing moved its headquarters to San Rafael in 1984, its newly completed 60,000-square-foot facility provided visible evidence of the company's dynamic evolution in Marin County. The firm had grown from modest beginnings to become a major national source of financing for high-technology equipment and associated enterprises.

The founding partner of Phoenix Leasing, Gus Constantin, is chairman and chief executive officer of the Phoenix companies, and a longtime resident of San Rafael. His seminal concept, born some 15 years ago, was to purchase high-technology and other specialized equipment with equity raised from limited partnerships. Equipment would not be acquired unless there was a lease agreement ready to be put into effect. The benefits of this approach are threefold—the manufacturer has a cash sale, the end-user leasing the equipment has immediate access to the latest technology, while the objective for the investor is substantial, predictable income.

Since 1972 Phoenix has established almost 30 limited partnerships and acquired more than one billion dollars of leased high-technology equipment for investor portfolios. This equipment is purchased from a wide variety of top-rated manufacturers and ranges from computer mainframes to small business systems. Equipment lessees are largely *Fortune* 1,000 companies and government agencies.

The success of Constantin's concept is borne out in the history of the growth of Phoenix' operations. Shortly after its founding in 1972, the fledgling company rented office space in Sausalito. At that time there was a staff of four. By 1980 Phoenix had built and occupied new offices in Mill Valley. Even though this building has been designed to accommodate 60 people, the fast-growing company was once again forced to seek more space, resulting in the move to San Rafael. The two-story building on four acres between Kerner and Francisco boulevards supports more than 20 satellite offices across the country and is headquarters for more than 250 employees nationwide.

As Phoenix grew, so did the diversity of its services. While the backbone of the firm's business remains in leasing computer mainframes and peripherals, Phoenix has created opportunities in related areas. In addition to direct leasing, Phoenix works with individual manufacturers to develop private-label programs. The company also saw a need for helping provide smaller business systems, and was one of the first to offer software-only leases.

Phoenix' knowledge of the cable television industry has led to its taking an active role in financing expansion and improvement of existing cable systems. It also purchases and operates some smaller systems that show growth potential.

High-technology and entrepreneurial activity are almost synonymous. Phoenix has taken a special interest in helping emerging companies supported by the venture capital community bring their products to the marketplace.

Multifaceted activities require multifaceted talents from operational staff. You'll find Phoenix personnel with expertise in accounting, finance, lease marketing and administration, partnership marketing and administration, equipment marketing, legal services, data and word processing, systems development, corporate communications, and office services.

Phoenix is a key presence in the planned development of East San Rafael, and the company has taken a keen interest in all elements contributing to the ongoing viability of the city's master plan. One of the top 10 employers in Marin County, Phoenix has been a primary sponsor of the shuttle service linking East and Downtown San Rafael, and of bus lines providing express commute service from Novato and Petaluma.

Phoenix became a public company in 1982; the parent company, Phoenix American Incorporated, is traded on the NASDAQ National Market System under the symbol PHXA. Phoenix Leasing Incorporated is a wholly owned subsidiary of Phoenix American, as is Phoenix Securities, Inc. Other affiliates are Phoenix Cable, Phoenix Venture, and Phoenix Micro-Systems Leasing.

Ranked among the top 10 employers in San Rafael, Phoenix American Incorporated provides its employees with a pleasant environment in which to work at its 2401 Kerner Boulevard location.

SAN RAFAEL JOE'S

One of Marin's oldest and most popular restaurants is located in the heart of downtown San Rafael at 931 Fourth Street. Known for its old-style Italian cooking, modest prices, and convivial atmosphere, San Rafael Joe's has become a veritable Fourth Street institution since it first opened in 1947.

The guiding force behind the restaurant has been the Farina family, part owners since 1950 and sole owners since 1980. Theresa and Guido Farina came to America in 1939 and 1949, respectively, but did not meet until 1950 in San Francisco. In a matter of months they became partners in marriage and in business, joining with Hector and Nancy Rubini to create the long-standing tradition of Joe's over the next 30 years.

Since 1950 the restaurant has more than tripled in size. In 1950 Joe's

Since 1947 Marin has enjoyed the old-style Italian atmosphere and cooking of San Rafael Joe's, a restaurant guided by the Farina family. Pictured here is the new banquet room that accommodates up to 125 people.

had a seating capacity of 100. Today, after several expansions and remodelings of adjoining areas, the restaurant can comfortably seat 200 people, with an adjacent banquet room that can easily accommodate another 125 people for business functions and private parties.

As Joe's has grown in space and popularity, so has the Farina family's participation in the restaurant. Guido and Theresa's nephew, Ches Bornia, has been with Joe's for 18 years; their son, Carlo Farina, for 15 years. Together this second generation of the family runs the entire kitchen operation, while Guido and Theresa manage the front office, hosting, and banquet room responsibilities. It is not an exaggeration to say that Joe's and the Farina family are inseparable.

With a staff of 60, San Rafael Joe's is open from 11 a.m. to 2 a.m. six days a week, and serves more than 1,000 people every day. Lunch-hour patrons count on Joe's for consistent, high-quality food and quick service. Authentic Italian dinners are served on elegant linen tablecloths at a leisurely

pace. And late-night diners can count on Joe's for a meal or a nightcap to top off an evening at the theater.

Joe's new banquet facility, opened in September 1986, hosts business conferences, private parties, receptions, and weddings. The Rotary Club, Kiwanis Club, chamber of commerce, and other local organizations hold regular luncheons and dinners at Joe's. A cozy adjoining room, filled with fine Italian and California wines, offers privacy for smaller functions.

Over the years Joe's has played an important role in San Rafael's civic and charitable activities. The restaurant has contributed dinners, food, and funds to many local organizations, including the Boy Scouts, Little League, the *Independent Journal*'s homeless fund during the winter storms of 1982, and many others.

Longtime traditions like Joe's do not materialize overnight, of course. They take hard work, consistently fine food and service, and, most important, *dedication*—in the case of San Rafael Joe's, a family's 38 years of dedication to a restaurant and a community.

MARIN GENERAL HOSPITAL

Once a resort hotel offering rest and relaxation among the swaying palms of Greenbrae, Marin General is now a highly respected community hospital offering quality health care in the same centrally located Marin County setting.

Marin General had its origin in the midst of a hospital crisis. The year was 1945: Many veterans were returning home from the war, the postwar baby boom was just beginning, and the county was in dire need of a new hospital facility.

"During the war and then afterward, we explored several ways to finance a new hospital," recalls Howard Hammond, M.D., who worked actively during this period and is now a retired member of the Marin General staff. "During the war this effort was led by doctors W.S. Pollard, Harold Fletcher, and Carl Clark, and after the war by Wilson Goddard and Harry Hensler. We formed local committees to promote a hospital district. A number of local citizens also volunteered their time and energy, including Phil Kennedy, John O'Connell, Herman Hale, Marian Ibach, Boyd Stewart, and Harold Riede."

One of these concerned committees was the Marin Postwar Planning Committee. When the health department issued a report in 1945, recommending construction of a 100-bed hospital in Marin, the committee determined it was time to take action. A hospital district was formed, and a bond issue—combined with federal and state funding—provided the money to build the facility. By 1950 the architectural plans were drawn, building contracts were negotiated, and ground was broken on the site of the old Bon Air Hotel.

A bronze plaque hanging in the entrance of the institution proudly displays the names of the elected directors who saw the project through to its completion in May 1952: Kennedy, O'Connell, Hale, Ibach, and Edwin B. Smith. From the beginning community members have committed both their time and money to Marin General. In 1963 contributions from the William Babcock Memorial Foundation and the C.T. Gruenhagen family helped to build a new wing with an additional 100 beds, California's first 12-bed heart unit, a cobalt therapy unit, and an intensive care unit. Shortly thereafter, psychiatric care services and a hearing and speech center were established. In 1968 the Community Mental Health Center, a joint effort with Marin County, was opened, in part due to the leadership of E.N. Kettenhofen.

Today Marin General Hospital reflects a new generation of medical care. The founders' vision of using advanced medical technology and personalized care to enhance both the length and quality of life has been achieved. New educational and preventive medicine programs improve the health of the

Advanced medical technology and personalized care, both staff and volunteer, come together at Marin General Hospital, where specialized health services are provided at all stages of life.

Marin General Hospital, located at 250 Bon Air Road in Greenbrae, offers a wide range of quality health care services to the communities of Marin County.

community through personal awareness and self-care. The institution's wide range of services provide health care throughout all stages of life: The Family Birth Center offers several birth options, all in private-room settings; the Adolescent Recovery Center gives teens with alcohol and drug problems a chance for a new beginning; and the hospital's specially accredited cancer program combines treatment in the oncology and radiation therapy departments.

A major addition to the hospital in 1988 will expand its surgical, intensive care, and coronary care services. The hospital's cardiac catheterization laboratory opened in 1986. Growing and changing with the needs of its patients, Marin General Hospital continues to meet its commitment to the community as a high-quality, full-service, non-profit hospital.

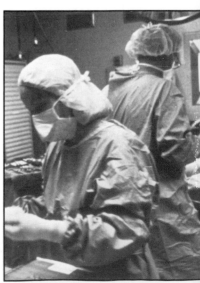

MARIN SURPLUS

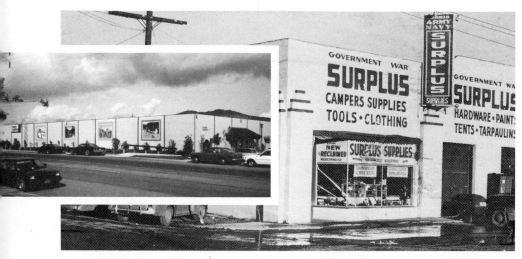

The original store, Marin Army Navy Surplus Supplies, opened in 1946 at 601 Francisco Boulevard, and (inset) the present-day Marin Surplus store at Simms Street and Andersen Boulevard in San Rafael.

Over the past three decades the popularity of camping, backpacking, and other outdoor activities has increased dramatically, particularly in Marin County where people appreciate the natural environment. As interest in the outdoors has grown, so has Marin Surplus, Northern California's major outlet for outdoor gear.

Founded in October 1946 by brothers-in-law Burt Capel and Harry Friedman, the original store was located at 601 Francisco Boulevard, at that time in the tidelands area on the outskirts of San Rafael. As the store's business prospered—and the Canal Area overflowed several times, flooding the store—it was clearly time to acquire a new facility. In 1956 the company moved to a larger building at 933 Francisco Boulevard, and in 10 years moved again to its present location at Simms and Andersen streets. Today, after two large-scale expansions, Marin Surplus occupies more than 35,000 square feet of space in its San Rafael headquarters and has three other stores in Petaluma, Santa Rosa, and Fairfield, and a new distribution center in Petaluma.

The company has adapted and diversified its merchandise lines to suit the needs of its customers. Originally, hardware comprised the bulk of the store's inventory, stocked with government surplus items from Hamilton Air

George Wayfer (left), shown here with founder Burt Capel, is manager of sales and training and has been with the company since 1953.

Force Base and other military installations. Marin Surplus continues to carry tools, telescopes, binoculars, knives, and other hardware, but now also offers a wide variety of tents, sleeping bags, backpacks, tarps, shoes, jackets, and durable clothing for men and women. In addition, the store carries a wide range of government surplus from other countries, such as field jackets, canteens, and duffel bags from European countries and Australia, and a number of hard-to-find and out-of-season items, such as suitcase handles, tally counters, and pocket scissors. What Marin Surplus doesn't have on hand, it will try to special order from its many resources.

The success of the store may be attributed not only to a wide selection of merchandise, but also to service. When most retailers have trimmed their staffs or have gone to self-service,

Marin Surplus has moved in the opposite direction: Courteous, knowledgeable, and thoroughly trained salespeople are always available to offer advice and suggestions. Marin Surplus stores have roomy, well-lighted aisles for browsing, and free coffee is always on hand in a homey, friendly "general store" atmosphere.

People have been drawn to Marin Surplus during storms, floods, power blackouts, and other emergency situations. In 1981 a heavy winter storm forced employees and customers to spend a night on the store's balcony. The store's expertise in disaster situations led the American Red Cross to ask the organization to develop a disaster plan to serve as a model for other businesses and disaster survival kits, sold in the stores.

Marin Surplus has been family owned and operated since its founding. In 1960 Burt Capel's son-in-law, John Meyer, joined the firm; much of the company's growth can be attributed to his service-oriented philosophy, employee cash-incentive programs, and community involvement. Meyer, the company's president, has worked actively with local youth groups, schools, and scholarship programs in San Rafael and throughout Marin County. Capel's other son-in-law, David Mayer, entered the company in 1973 as buyer of clothing. Daniel Mayer, Burt Capel's grandson, has been in the business since 1970, and is manager of company operations.

For more than 40 years the community has relied on Marin Surplus for all its outdoor needs. Because of its dedication to serving customers and its proven ability to keep up with the times, its future appears even more promising, both for the community and the company's 135 employees.

MARIN CLEANERS

Through the years dry cleaning and laundering have become specialized operations requiring meticulous attention to detail, vigilant care, and modern machinery. With 35 years and three generations in the textile cleaning business, Marin Cleaners has successfully melded these aspects to evolve into the largest family dry cleaning-laundry operation in Marin County.

Marin Cleaners was founded in 1952 by Bert and Lucille Brown, who had been in the dry cleaning business in San Francisco and Petaluma since shortly after World War II. The Browns opened the first Marin Cleaners store, an 1,800-square-foot facility, at 716 Fourth Street; but the operation soon outgrew its environs and moved to a 3,000-square-foot plant a block away at 520 Fourth Street—one of the company's three present locations.

The Browns' two sons, Ronald and Robert Cassasa, were active in the family business almost from the beginning. In 1957 they purchased a small press shop in the Cove Shopping Center in Tiburon. Over the next 15 years they developed the laundry side of the operation, finally opening another new facility to handle laundry in 1973.

Today Marin Cleaners is a full-service, highly automated operation with two totally computerized dry cleaning units. Headquartered at 700 A Street, the company employs 60 people at three different locations, including the Tiburon store, which has doubled in size and is Marin Cleaners' highest volume store. And the third generation of the family, Robert's sons William and Gary, have entered the business. William manages the Tiburon outlet, and Gary runs the Fourth Street store in San Rafael.

From a $140,000 annual sales volume in 1952, the company now realizes $2 million annually. In addition to the retail side of the business, Marin

Cleaners also handles the laundry operations for 15 smaller dry cleaning outlets in the county.

The reason for the success of the company is simple—customer satisfaction. Most of the firm's customers are gained from word of mouth, a sure sign that the name "Marin Cleaners" is trusted throughout the community. In addition, Marin families need not go to several different stores to fulfill their textile needs—Marin Cleaners' full-service approach can handle all types of dry cleaning, laundering, reweaving, and sewing.

The Cassasas have long been leaders in the textile industry, and they travel extensively to conventions and trade shows to keep up with the latest

technology and techniques. Ronald is secretary/treasurer of the Textile Service Industry Association in Northern California; Robert has been an officer in the state association of the California Fabricare Institute (CFI); William is currently director of the NIDC in the North Bay; and Gary is sergeant at arms in the same association.

Ronald and Robert Cassasa are planning to retire soon and turn over the reins of the company to William and Gary. With 35 years of dry cleaning and laundering experience in their blood, it should be an easy transition.

Bert and Lucille Brown opened the new Marin Cleaners at 520 Fourth Street in 1955.

The new facility featured off-street parking and was almost twice the size of the original store.

CITY OF SAN RAFAEL

When longtime San Rafael residents reminisce about the "good old days," they usually think of the venerable old homes, white picket fences, and giant shade trees that lined the city's streets in the 1920s and 1930s. However, just 50 years earlier—before it was even incorporated as a town—San Rafael was a dusty, dirty, and often free-swinging American frontier community.

Cattle roamed the streets unmolested. The few trees in the village were dry and spindly. Loggers, cattle drivers, and gold rushers burst into town, stopped long enough to buy a few whiskeys and some feed for their animals, and moved quickly on, usually to San Francisco. In those days almost everything about the hamlet depended on San Francisco. San Rafael's first railroad, completed in 1870, was built to connect the village to the Point San Quentin ferry, which would take the travelers and their beef and lumber to the growing "metropolis" across the bay.

In the early 1870s its civic leaders recognized that if San Rafael were ever to forge its own identity, it would need its own laws, fire protection, and police protection—in short, its own government. After several editorials appeared in the *Marin County Journal* advocating San Rafael's incorporation as a town, a committee was appointed to draft an incorporation bill. The bill was passed by the state legislature in January 1874, and on February 18, 1874, the town of San Rafael was born.

The town's first official election was held two months later when San Rafael voters elected its first board of trustees, the predecessor of today's city council. During its first year the board hired a gun-toting marshal to keep the peace, installed gaslights along the streets, established a volunteer hose company (the forerunner of today's fire department), and purchased $1,000 worth of fire-fighting equipment.

The next year the town government was able to scrape up enough funds to move to San Rafael's first town hall, a small building on the west side of C Street leased at $30 a month from Isaac Shaver, a lumber mill owner. The trustees began to shape a new city as people stopped passing through San Rafael and began to stay. Its population increased almost fourfold, from 600 in 1874 to 2,276 by 1880.

A decade later the town's population had grown to 3,000, automatically qualifying it for status as a city. The first city election was held in 1893; 577 of its 704 registered voters turned up at the polls. The community had also earned a reputation as a resort; the grand Hotel Rafael, built in 1888, attracted San Franciscans and tourists from around the world.

San Rafael changed physically, due to the efforts of city officials and civic groups. The San Rafael Improvement Club, a women's group organized in 1902, planted thousands of trees along the town's streets. Gordon's Opera House at Fourth and D—the scene of many local Shakespearean productions, political rallies, and high school graduations during the last decade of the nineteenth century—became the community's first movie house, the Lyric Theatre, in 1902. A rival theater, the Palm, opened across the street six years later.

The event that would have the most significant effect upon the early growth of San Rafael happened, as one might expect, in San Francisco—the Great Earthquake of 1906. As hundreds of quake refugees fled to Marin, city officials helped to distribute money, food, and clothing to the homeless—many of whom stayed permanently in San Rafael.

In 1908, with the city's population

Fourth Street, downtown San Rafael. Photo by Tom Lolini

San Rafael Canal at the mouth of the San Rafael Slough. Photo by Tom Lolini

Mission San Rafael de Archangel. Photo by Tom Lolini

ballooning to 6,500, local government built its first city hall at Fifth Avenue and A Street, a structure that would serve as the seat of city government for 58 years. Today's San Rafael Public Library was built that same year from funds provided by the Carnegie Foundation. San Rafael voters in 1910 adopted a city charter, making San Rafael the first—and still only—city in Marin County with a charter form of government.

The Roaring '20s began with a flu epidemic and ended in a roaring blaze. At the request of civic leaders, Red Cross volunteers and Dominican Sisters provided emergency care for flu victims at the Hotel Rafael in 1920. Eight years later the hotel burned to the ground, all but ending San Rafael's tradition as the elite resort of Marin County.

The Great Depression hurt San Rafael economically, but not nearly as much as many other areas of the country. For one thing, San Rafael's labor population was not high; perhaps more important, the farsighted efforts of city government were able to mitigate many disastrous consequences. The city played a major role in supporting the construction of the Golden Gate

Bridge and Hamilton Air Field. The bridge, completed in 1937, brought in a large influx of San Francisco commerce, and Hamilton brought stable, salaried, military personnel to the area.

The outbreak of World War II sparked another population surge for San Rafael, when workers streamed into Marin to build the Kaiser Liberty ships in Sausalito. After the war many of these workers and their families, and many former Hamilton Army personnel, settled in San Rafael. New subdivisions and developments sprouted on the outskirts of the community, expanding its boundaries north to Terra Linda—which was annexed in 1973—and east into Loch Lomond, Glenwood, and Peacock Gap. By 1960 the city's population had passed 20,000, up dramatically from 8,500 in 1940.

In 1966 San Rafael built a $1.1-million city hall at 1400 Fifth Avenue, the present seat of local government. Other city-owned buildings include the former Dollar Mansion, now called the Falkirk Cultural Center; the Boyd House, leased to the Marin County Historical Society; seven fire stations; three recreation centers; and the San Rafael Public Library.

Since 1970 city government has

The Falkirk Cultural Center.

followed the open space acquisition policy mandated by San Rafael voters in several elections, referenda, and bond issues, preserving the scenic environment that residents have come to value so highly over the years. At the same time the city has sought to stimulate the financial vitality of San Rafael business districts with a special Redevelopment Agency created in 1972.

With 335 full-time employees the City of San Rafael offers the complete range of modern civic services. In the coming years the community will strive to maintain its position as the retail and commercial hub of Marin County, while simultaneously conserving the high quality of life that has been San Rafael's trademark since its incorporation 114 years ago.

San Pablo Bay. Photo by Tom Lolini

EDWIN G. IMHAUS COMPANY

The terms "creative" and "insurance broker" are seldom uttered in the same sentence, but the Edwin G. Imhaus Company has combined the two successfully for more than a half-century. Insurance and creativity go back four generations in the Imhaus family—all the way to the turn of the century, when Alfred E. and Laura Imhaus first started in the business.

Alfred was the manager of the San Francisco-based General Insurance Company at the time—and first clarinetist of the San Francisco Symphony. His wife, Laura, was one of the first Bay Area women to obtain an insurance broker's license and start her own insurance venture—a strikingly creative achievement in the presuffrage era.

Their son, Edwin G. Imhaus, founded the present company in San Francisco in 1927. An extremely talented operatic tenor, Edwin gave up the chance to train at the renowned La Scala Opera House in order to pursue a career in the insurance business. Although insurance was his primary endeavor, Edwin never abandoned his singing: He performed on the radio, in concerts, and in many San Francisco Bohemian Club productions throughout his life. Many Bay Area football fans can still recall his powerful renditions of the "Star Spangled Banner," which he sang before Shrine East-West games at Stanford Stadium for 37 years.

When Edwin died in 1966 the next generation, Ron and Susanne Hill Imhaus, took over the reins of the company and continued to use the family's creative instincts in the insurance business. One of the first things they did was to move the firm to San Rafael in 1972—an innovative move in those days and a much-imitated one in the years following, as many other organizations discovered the benefits of relocating in Marin County. During the 1970s Susanne assumed more responsibility for the company's operations

The Edwin G. Imhaus Company staff (from left) are Conrad Imhaus, president; Geri Ryan; Susanne Imhaus, chairman and chief executive officer; Candy Hajek; Dion Downs; Pat Lehman; and Gregg Cappel.

and became chairman and chief executive officer after Ron's death in 1985, bringing the insurance legacy of Laura Imhaus full circle.

Meanwhile, the fourth generation of the founding family, Conrad Imhaus, had joined the company after graduating cum laude from the University of San Francisco. Continuing the tradition of community involvement established by his grandfather, Conrad is active in the San Rafael Elks Club, Rotary Club, chamber of commerce, the San Francisco Boy's and Girl's clubs, the Olympic Club, the Press Club, and the Guardsmen, a group of under-40 businessmen who conduct fund-raising drives for disadvantaged children. Susanne has served as president of the Zonta Club, a women's professional organization, and as a director on the board of the San Rafael Chamber of Commerce.

Today the Edwin G. Imhaus Company is a thriving full-service insurance brokerage. Over the years the organization's reputation as a creative agent has been enhanced by its solutions for "problem cases": organizations and programs that have difficulty finding affordable coverage due to skyrocketing premium rates and industry trends.

With an expert staff of 10 employees and an annual premium volume of almost $10 million, the Edwin G. Imhaus Company continues to grow internally, mandating a move from its longtime location at 4340 Redwood Highway to a more spacious facility in the near future. With its steady stream of innovative solutions to all types of business and personal insurance problems, the firm will continue to be a vital, creative force in Marin County for years to come.

ANDREW JAMES RING III, AIA, ARCHITECT, INC.

San Rafael has its fair share of building craftsmen, but none more prolific nor more well known throughout the state than architect Jim Ring. Over a 20-year span his firm has designed more than 600 commercial and residential properties in California.

Ring founded his architect's practice in San Francisco in 1967. While most young architects join established firms after completing their apprenticeships, Ring always wanted to be out on his own as an independent. As it turned out, his self-confidence was justified: In less than two years he had earned a reputation as a designer of

commercial buildings on the San Francisco waterfront and of office interiors in the city's downtown financial district. In fact, he was well on his way to forging his own established firm, employing 15 people by 1970.

The organization moved to Marin in 1971, and since that time it has designed more than 200 buildings in the county, including the Marin *Independent Journal* building, First National Bank of Marin (formerly San Rafael Cottage Hospital), California Federal Savings and Loan, Jandy Industries' corporate headquarters and manufacturing plant, Transworld Systems, California Financial Park, extensive remodeling for the corporate headquarters of the First Federal Savings and Loan Association, and a proposed

100 Tamal Plaza in Corte Madera.

$23-million hotel development for the Ghilotti family.

Long before other architects were designing housing for the elderly, Ring was a specialist in the field. His retirement community developments, such as Rotary Manor and Lamplighters, are considered by experts to be prototypical designs for functional, aesthetic, low-cost housing for senior citizens.

The firm is renowned for its imagination and creativity, particularly in situations of tight budget constraints. A typical Jim Ring design emphasizes the human element and blends in perfectly with the natural environment, while still maintaining the structural integrity and functional requirements of the project.

As might be expected, both Ring and his practice have been extremely active in San Rafael's civic and business affairs. A former president of the San Rafael Chamber of Commerce, he is a member of the San Rafael Rotary Club, president of the San Rafael Public Education Foundation, a member of the executive board of the Marin Council of the Boy Scouts of America, and a leader on many citizens' action committees.

Andrew James Ring III, AIA, Architect, Inc., is a major contributor to the physical growth of San Rafael and its attractiveness as a modern commercial center.

First National Bank of Marin.

MOUNT TAMALPAIS CEMETERY AND MORTUARY

The Mount Tamalpais Cemetery as seen from the surrounding Marin hills. Photo circa 1920

The history of Mount Tamalpais Cemetery and Mortuary goes back more than a century. In 1878 a group of San Rafael men met to survey a large plot of serene, lush land owned by Alfred W. Dubois. A sheepherder and scientific researcher, Dubois agreed to use his land for a cemetery when several of his San Rafael neighbors objected to his experiments.

The group laid out roads and drew up a topographical map of the 120-acre area at the top of Fifth Avenue. In 1880 Mount Tamalpais Cemetery was formally dedicated and held the first meeting of its new board of directors: president J.O. Eldridge, vice-president A.C. Nichols, treasurer A.M. Gardou, secretary Alfred W. Dubois, comptroller Henry A. Dubois (Alfred's son), and legal counsel T.G. Newland.

The early years of the cemetery were as quiet as the green hills surrounding it. (In fact, only 5,000 burials were conducted during its first 70 years.) By 1910, however, the City of San Rafael was interested in purchasing some of the cemetery's land, and an agreement was reached whereby the city ceded 63 acres and paid the Dubois family $12,350.

Through the first half of the twentieth century—despite two world wars and the Great Depression—the cemetery was stable, secure, and financially sound. As a nonprofit organization, Mount Tamalpais was run by a board of directors who were elected by lotholders owning 200 square feet of cemetery property. Its clientele were (and still are) some of the most prominent families in the Bay Area, such as the Diblees, Kibbles, Dollars, and Mailliards.

In the early 1950s two events occurred that would later prove to have profound impact on Mount Tamalpais' future. In 1952 Weston L. Roe joined the organization as cemetery manager. Originally from Logan, Utah, Roe had been in the funeral and cemetery business since 1946 before moving to San Francisco. He retired in June 1987, and his expertise and courteous manner have been the hallmark of the cemetery's continuity for 35 years.

The second event was a change of ownership and management to the Cypress Abbey Company in 1954. Cypress Abbey had 50 years' experience in operating cemeteries in the Bay Area, including Cypress Lawn Memorial Park, Olivet Memorial Park, Greenlawn Memorial Park (all in Colma), and the Memorial Columbarium in San Francisco. At that point Mount Tamalpais became a profit-making organization, and, with a big spurt in growth in Marin County population, its business began to expand under Roe's guidance and leadership.

New offices were constructed, and the original mausoleum, built in 1922, was expanded. In the 1960s Marin's first crematorium was completed at the cemetery; four additional mausoleums were also erected, providing many more crypts and niches. Many new lawn areas, gardens, trees, and shrubberies were planted.

Mount Tamalpais experienced another transition when the Marin County Cemetery Company, under president Buck Kamphausen, took over ownership in 1981. With long experience in cemetery and funeral home management, Kamphausen and the company also operate Skyview Memorial Lawn in Vallejo, Chapel of the Light in Fresno, Fairfield Funeral Home in Fairfield, and Evergreen Cemetery in Oakland. In 1983 the Mount Tamalpais Mortuary opened on the same grounds as the cemetery. Under the expert guidance of mortuary manager Bill Miller, the facility provides the highest quality funeral home services.

Today the Mount Tamalpais Cemetery and Mortuary staff of eight employees offer sensitive, personalized service to meet the full range of funeral and gravesite needs. The staff consults with family and clergy, offers complete administrative and clerical services (including preparation of death certificates and assistance with union or insurance documents), and makes comprehensive plans for funeral and memorial services.

Mount Tamalpais is fully equipped to handle either cremation or burial. A full line of caskets and urns are offered in a wide variety of woods, metals, and fabrics to meet the needs of every family budget. Despite the presence of several prominent families, the cemetery's rates are very competitive and well within the means of the average family.

All religious denominations are accepted.

Most people now provide for their family's burial estate well in advance, thereby assuring a location of their own choice and avoiding the needless infliction of this duty upon loved ones during life's most anguished moments. Mount Tamalpais is there to assist in this important responsibility.

Marin County has changed a great deal over the past 100 years, but the Mount Tamalpais grounds remain almost unchanged in the same secluded, historic setting where it began more than a century ago. San Rafael can be proud of Mount Tamalpais Cemetery and Mortuary—it would be difficult to find a final resting place with more dignity and beauty.

The entrance to Mount Tamalpais Cemetery and Mortuary, circa 1900.

KAISER PERMANENTE

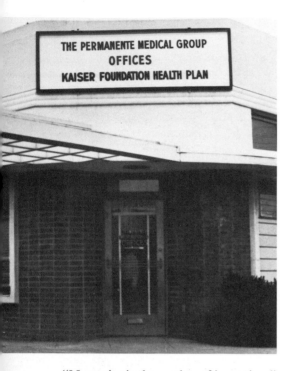

"Necessity is the mother of invention," claims the old proverb, and nowhere was this relation more graphically illustrated than in the origin of Kaiser Permanente, the nation's largest private prepaid group practice health care program.

The year was 1933 and the place was the Mojave Desert in Southern California, where 5,000 workers were building the Los Angeles Aqueduct. The "necessity" was local medical

The first Marin location for Kaiser Permanente was at 1930 Fourth Street in San Rafael in 1958.

care, which the workers almost completely lacked—if a worker was hurt on the construction project there was no alternative but to send him back to Los Angeles for medical attention.

To the rescue came Sidney Garfield, M.D., a young Los Angeles surgeon who built a small hospital on skids that could follow the workers as they progressed across the desert. Though the hospital had only 10 beds, it offered a modern operating room and laboratory, X-ray equipment, comfortable surroundings, and a highly qualified medical staff. The Depression-era workers were thrilled with the new facility; but they had one major problem—they could not afford the costs of treatment. Understandably, the hospital soon ran into financial difficulties and would have been forced to close if Garfield had not come up with a reasonable solution.

Dr. Garfield's "invention" was the direct predecessor of today's group practice prepayment plan—each worker contributed five cents per day from his payroll check and, combined with a similar amount from worker's compensation premiums, industrial and

nonindustrial medical coverage was ensured. In a short time 95 percent of the workers had enrolled in the program, and the hospital survived.

Garfield's plan was so successful that five years later Henry and Edgar Kaiser asked him to establish a similar health plan for Kaiser workers and their families at the equally remote Grand Coulee Dam construction site in Washington. Again the plan was offered on a voluntary basis to workers at a rate of 50 cents per week. Within one month 90 percent of the workers and their families had joined the program.

The plan was revolutionary from both the administrative and clinical viewpoints. Administratively, the financial risk of illness and injury was spread among the enrolled families at costs they could easily afford. And the plan's "fixed-revenue" approach meant that the program's physicians could design, organize, and budget facilities and services effectively and efficiently.

Clinically, the program had a significant impact on the way medicine was practiced. Until that time physicians had relied on sick and injured patients to make a living; afterward doctors had a vested interest in keeping them well. The fact that Kaiser Permanente Health Plan members could get care without worrying about the cost profoundly affected the general health of the community: Members came to the physicians earlier in their illnesses, resulting in easier, more effective, and less costly treatment.

By 1942 the Kaiser family was sold on the idea of the group practice prepayment plan and called on Garfield to organize a program for workers at the Kaiser shipyards in Richmond, California, and Vancouver, Washington, and at a Kaiser steel mill in Fontana,

The Terra Linda Valley Hospital was purchased in 1966 by Kaiser Permanente.

The present location of Kaiser Permanente Medical Center at 99 Montecillo Road in San Rafael.

California. The United States had entered World War II, thousands of workers had migrated to these areas to build the Kaiser "liberty ships," and existing medical facilities were just not adequate.

Kaiser set up six medical field stations in Richmond and took over the 54-bed Fabiola Hospital in Oakland, thus establishing the first Permanente Foundation hospital. At these facilities the plan once again emphasized a new dimension of health care—preventive medicine. A public health committee was formed to control communicable diseases. A shipyard loudspeaker system, previously used only for entertainment, became a medium for informing workers about important health programs. And a cancer detection clinic was developed for women as part of Kaiser's gynecological services. At the peak of wartime shipbuilding the plan served the needs of 200,000 members, proving that the plan could work in urban as well as rural settings.

After the war, as the shipyards began to shut down, many of the workers wanted to continue their membership. Kaiser and Dr. Garfield agreed to con-

tinue the plan and open the program on a voluntary enrollment basis to the general community. In 1946 Kaiser Permanente entered its new era with 25,000 "charter members" in the San Francisco Bay Area, Portland-Vancouver, and Fontana, California.

During the 1950s Kaiser Permanente expanded to Los Angeles and Hawaii, and in the 1960s, to a truly national scale. By 1970 membership had increased one hundredfold to 2.5 million, and Kaiser Permanente had opened facilities in Cleveland, Denver, Sacramento, and San Diego. Kaiser Permanente is considered the model for the health maintenance organizations (HMOs), actively promoted by the federal government as an effective way to provide quality health care at a reasonable cost.

Today Kaiser Permanente is the nation's largest HMO, serving some five million members in 16 states and the District of Columbia. More than 5,800 physicians and 50,500 support staff provide health care through 28 hospital-based medical centers and 140 medical offices.

The San Rafael Medical Center,

located on Montecillo Road, is one of 14 hospital-based facilities in Kaiser Permanente's Northern California region. The center began in 1958 as a small clinic on Fourth Street in downtown San Rafael with a staff of three doctors, one nurse, and an office clerk. The clinic offered health care services in general medicine, internal medicine, and pediatrics, as well as laboratory and pharmacy services.

In less than two years the size of the staff had increased to 17, and the number of patients had increased from a few hundred to thousands. In the early 1960s a second floor and two other San Rafael buildings were acquired to meet the needs of additional services and patients.

In 1966 Kaiser Permanente purchased Terra Linda Valley Hospital, making it the 18th Kaiser Foundation Hospital nationwide and the 10th in the Northern California region. In late 1971 a major construction project was started to combine all community services at the Montecillo Road hospital location. Within five years the goal was achieved with the opening of the San Rafael Medical Center—a five-story ultramodern hospital and an adjacent five-story medical offices building.

The new hospital had 92 beds, including an eight-bed Intensive Care/Coronary Care Unit, and also offered a greatly expanded Emergency Department. In 1978 the medical offices building was expanded, adding 17 doctors' offices, 36 examination rooms, and a telephone advice center.

Today Kaiser's San Rafael facility serves more than 127,000 health plan members. The hospital has a 120-bed capacity and a newly redesigned ICU/CCU Department. More than 100 physicians and a staff of 850 care for the needs of San Rafael and the entire Marin County community.

DOMINIC'S HARBOR RESTAURANT

History sometimes repeats itself in delightful ways. Legend has it that in 1839 a young Irish-Italian cabin boy named Dominic Murphy was unhappy with his sailor's life and left his ship when it docked in San Francisco Bay. Only 15 years old at the time, Dominic was adopted by Spanish cattle herders who taught him all they knew about cooking and making fine wine. His talent for cooking soon gained him a formidable reputation: Spanish and American gentry and Yankee gold rushers came from miles around to taste the dishes prepared in his San Rafael kitchen.

Over a century later two Marin businessmen built a restaurant on the

Because Dominic's is situated right on the San Rafael Canal, diners can literally "sail in" to the restaurant.

The Dominic's Harbor Restaurant sign, a sky-borne boat named Le Filet *(The Net), is a Marin County landmark.*

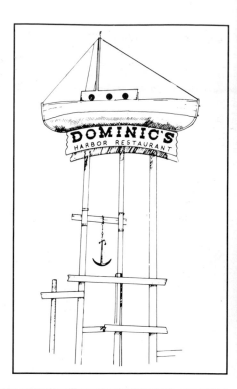

same site where Dominic Murphy once acted as chef and host and named it "Dominic's." In 1975 they sold the restaurant to a man who also had a rich background in cuisine and seafaring. The man's name: Dominic Pomilia!

The Pomilia family's history in navigation dates back to the early 1900s, when Dominic's father, Francesco Pomilia, immigrated from Sicily and became one of the pioneer commercial fishermen on San Francisco's Fisherman's Wharf. Francesco and his 16-foot sailboat (named, you guessed it, the *Dominic*) turned out to be the beginning of the largest fishing family in the Bay Area. Dominic's uncle

One of the Pomilia family's fishing boats heads out to sea to catch some of the fresh seafood served at Dominic's.

owned one of the first crab stands on Fisherman's Wharf. And Dominic's three brothers, Vito, Joe, and Frank, have skippered their own fishing boats for years and today still catch much of the fresh seafood served at Dominic's.

Today Dominic's Harbor Restaurant, owned and operated by the Pomilia family, is renowned for its gourmet food, fine wine, and traditional California hospitality. The restaurant's location on the San Rafael Canal offers a relaxed marine setting to complement the culinary arts of its world-famous chefs.

Known as "Marin's favorite rendezvous," Dominic's has always been more than a restaurant. Its banquet fa-

cilities can accommodate up to 500 people in three separate banquet rooms, ideal for business conferences, seminars, private parties, fashion shows, weddings, and cocktail parties. The facilities include a stage, public address system, and other amenities necessary for effective business functions and successful parties.

Dominic's Galleria, a large terrace with parasol-crowned tables, affords pleasant, comfortable outdoor dining. Afternoon and evening cocktails are served in Dominic's L'Escale, a bar-lounge with a charming boat-like ambience. Before dinner guests may browse through the restaurant's wine room and choose a vintage California or European wine to enhance their luncheon or dinner selection.

Dominic's menu offers more than 60 delicious seafood and Italian specialties, many of which feature mesquite charcoal cooking. Over the years many celebrities from all fields have dined at the restaurant, including Vice-President George Bush, Joe Dimaggio, Paul Newman, and Clint Eastwood.

Dominic's has also won several culinary awards, most notably the Silver Spoon Award in 1982, 1985, 1986, and 1987, given by the Gourmet Diners Club of America for high-quality food and service.

Dominic's Harbor Restaurant serves lunch and dinner seven days a week. Special brunches are offered on Saturdays, Sundays, and holidays. Low-price "sunset" dinners are served Monday through Friday, 4:30 p.m. to 6:30 p.m.

Dominic Pomilia's brothers often kid him about being the restaurateur who "strayed from the sea." As with his namesake of more than a century ago, the sea's loss has been the landlubbers' gain.

CLARION HOTEL MARIN

Hospitality may be a forgotten word in today's frenetic world of business travel, but not at the Clarion Hotel Marin in San Rafael. Since the Clarion opened its doors in June 1984, it has built a reputation as a warm, relaxed "home away from home" for hundreds of commercial travelers. It provides comprehensive facilities for business meetings and conferences, and local group functions.

Located just off Highway 101 at 1010 Northgate Drive, the hotel property was originally constructed in 1969 as part of the Holiday Inn chain. The 100-room facility was expanded to its current 230-room size two years later.

Prior to its reopening in June 1984, the Clarion Hotel sign replaced the previous Holiday Inn sign.

Throughout the 1970s the inn primarily served vacation travelers, offering an "easy-access" location just minutes from San Francisco and close to Marin's fine ocean beaches and the Napa/Sonoma wine country.

In the early 1980s the Clarion's parent corporation, Associated Inns & Restaurants Company of America (AIRCOA), was searching for a Northern California property that could easily be converted to its new "Clarion Collection"—a line of full-service, commercial travel-oriented hotels that had just begun operations at 11 locations across the nation. With its elegant setting, ample parking facilities, and conference potential, the Northgate Drive property seemed a perfect choice.

Upon taking over the property

in 1984, AIRCOA immediately embarked on a lavish $1.7-million renovation program for its newest Clarion. Finished in the spring of 1987, the project completely remodeled existing facilities and added several new amenities designed with the business traveler in mind.

All 230 guest rooms were refurbished to include new color schemes, lighting, desks, bedding, draperies, and soundproofing. Seven deluxe combination suites were formed. In addition, the Clarion's unique Executive Registry level was established, offering special luxuries for members of the hotel's Executive Travelers Club as well as for travelers who desire upgraded accommodations. Club members receive express check-in/check-out privileges, preferred rates, upgrades to the best available rooms, free spousal stays, direct billing, and guaranteed reservations when made more than 72 hours in advance. The Clarion's Executive Registry also instituted concierge service to assist with travel arrangements, duplicating and typing, and other business functions.

The extensive remodeling included expansion of the hotel's banquet and meeting space. Seven meeting/banquet rooms, totaling 6,000 square feet, can now accommodate groups of 10 to 400 for business and social events. The largest room, the Bay Room, has almost 3,000 square feet and a seating capacity of 350 people theatre-style or 250 banquet-style. State-of-the-art audiovisual equipment was purchased to enhance presentations by conference and banquet speakers. The Clarion's fire-prevention, water-heating, and laundry equipment were upgraded to assure safety and efficient service to every room.

Andaron's Cafe, the hotel restaurant, was renovated in early 1987 and today seats 140 for breakfast, lunch,

The Clarion Hotel Marin nestles in the oak-st̶a̶t̶ hills of San Rafael.

and dinner. Well known for the quality of its food, the eatery has become a mainstay for guests and a popular lunch-hour retreat for the San Rafael business community. Andaron's Lounge, a popular nightspot, sparkles with quality entertainment and exciting guest-participation events.

The Clarion's 6.7 acres were landscaped with lush vegetation, and a new jacuzzi was installed to complement the hotel's heated courtyard pool.

San Rafael's city officials and business leaders supported the new facility from the beginning, and their commitment has been well rewarded. The city has benefited not only from the hotel's capital improvements but also from enhanced local employment and an increased tax base. The Clarion's 8-percent hotel occupancy tax goes directly to the city coffers. In addition, the hotel's new high-quality accommodations provide a comfortable

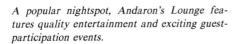

A popular nightspot, Andaron's Lounge features quality entertainment and exciting guest-participation events.

A lavish $1.7-million renovation program has just been finished. Shown here is the newly remodeled front lobby.

transition for people relocating to San Rafael.

Since its opening the establishment has evolved into a popular meeting facility for small and large companies alike, including many San Rafael and Marin County corporations. Fireman's Fund Insurance, WestAmerica Bank, Wells Fargo Bank, Micropro, and McGraw-Hill have all held regional sales conferences at the Clarion over the past three years.

The hotel's banquet facilities are in constant use by the local community. The San Rafael Chamber of Commerce, the San Rafael Rotary Club, and the Terra Linda Rotary Club are just a few of the local organizations that meet monthly at the Clarion.

Lush landscaping complements the Clarion's 6.7 acres, and a jacuzzi accompanies the hotel's heated courtyard pool.

The Clarion's parent corporation originated in Cleveland, Ohio, in 1968. The company grew rapidly in the early 1970s, establishing a reputation for identifying and developing unique opportunities in the hospitality industry. As an owner and developer of many properties, AIRCOA also managed several major franchise hotels, such as Sheratons, Hiltons, Holiday Inns, and Stouffer's. By the mid-1970s the firm had branched into tennis resorts, condominiums, ski lodges, vacation retreats, and convention facilities.

Headquartered in Englewood, Colorado, AIRCOA is currently one of the nation's largest hotel management and development organizations, with nearly 50 hotels, inns, resorts, and condominium properties located from Alaska to Mexico and from Maine to Hawaii. The company continues to manage several Hiltons and Sheratons as well as the new Wynfield Inns, a group of traditional mid-price inns located in Arizona, Colorado, Florida, and Utah. Employing 9,800 people and managing a total of 13,500 guest rooms, firms owned and operated by AIRCOA produced $300 million in revenues in 1985.

Meanwhile, the Clarion brand name has expanded to 24 properties. A new 300-room Clarion adjacent to Ontario Airport in Southern California features the most advanced high-tech conference facilities. On the shore of Anchorage's Lake Spenard, the world's busiest float plane base, Clarion erected a 248-room hotel. And the Clarion Hotel & Conference Center in Lansing, Michigan, boasts 26,000 square feet of public space, 300 rooms, and landscaped courtyards with pools, waterfalls, and fountains.

As a part of all this exciting growth, the Clarion Hotel Marin remains one of AIRCOA's showcase facilities. Nestled in the hills of Marin County, the hotel is just minutes from the cosmopolitan attractions of San Francisco, yet worlds apart from the city's bustle and congestion. Under superior management, the establishment has blossomed into San Rafael's only full-service hotel, complete with valet and room service, airport limousine service, gift shop, beauty salon, and Hertz Rental Car outlet.

Although its facilities and services are of the kind usually experienced in large urban hostelries, the Clarion Hotel Marin is most proud of its helpful "small inn" hospitality. Its expert staff provides professional assistance intended to make all business stays successful ones—from the "small touches," such as confections and cordials, to the large strategic preparations for meetings and conferences. The hospitality concept might have been forgotten by others in the industry, but it has been a watchword of this hotel's history, and will continue to be for years to come.

Emphasis has been placed on comprehensive facilities for business meetings and conferences, and local group functions. Shown here is one of seven meeting/banquet rooms, which can accommodate groups from 10 to 400.

KTIM AM/FM RADIO

Marin County's first—and only—radio station was founded by former Novato Mayor Hugh Turner in 1947. KTIM-AM broadcasts consisted primarily of the light musical fare of the period, interspersed with local news. In 1962 the Marin *Independent Journal* purchased the station from Turner, and, when FM was born in the early 1960s, the station began to "simulcast" programs on both AM and FM frequencies.

At about the same time a young man named Art Astor was working in radio advertising sales in Los Angeles. A native of Fresno, Astor had graduated from the University of Southern California with a degree in advertising and telecommunications. After a brief fling as a stand-up comedian and later as the host for a television music-dance show similar to "American Bandstand," he concluded that communications management—and someday owning his own facility—was his ultimate goal.

By the late 1960s Astor had attained the position of station manager for several Los Angeles radio stations: KHJ, KRTH, and KDAY. In the early 1970s he became executive vice-president of Drake-Chenault Enterprises, Inc., one of the largest radio production companies in the country. The firm also owned KIQQ-FM in Los Angeles. So when KIKF in Orange County was put up for sale in 1978, Astor was well prepared to realize his dream of ownership. In a few short years KIKF evolved into one of the leading country music stations in Southern California and enabled the new owner to look around for other properties.

Meanwhile, in Marin, KTIM was foundering under its then-owner Platt Communications, a group of investors who had purchased the station in 1980. In love with the Bay Area for many years and equally smitten by the station's "Big Band" AM format, Astor became the new owner of KTIM in 1983.

Today KTIM is truly the "Voice of Marin." The AM station (1510) plays a wide range of swing, jazz, and popular music from the 1930s to the 1980s. KTIM-FM (at 100.9) offers a blend of adult-oriented contemporary music. It also provides comprehensive world and local news, sports, business reports, and detailed weather and traffic updates.

KTIM is also a leader in public service and public affairs programming, offering several hours a week of public service programming and announcements of charitable and civic activities. Despite power blackouts throughout Marin during the harsh winter storms of recent years, the station continued to broadcast weather and road-closing bulletins—using an auxiliary generator.

"We're a community station," says Art Astor. "People here see us as their communication line to each other—as individuals and businesses."

The KTIM studios are located in an elegant, remodeled Victorian facility at 1623 Fifth Avenue in San Rafael. The station employs 25 people and broadcasts 24 hours a day on FM and

Art Astor, owner of KTIM AM/FM, with one specimen from his large collection of antique radios.

sunrise to sunset on AM. Although Art Astor still lives in Southern California, he commutes to San Rafael weekly and owns a local residence. The station's day-to-day operations are handled by general manager Susan Bice, general sales manager Victoria Mann, and business manager Nancy Barghini—all of whom have been with KTIM since 1983.

As far as the future is concerned, Astor states, "Our goal is to be an artistic success as well as a business success." This philosophy should result in many years of listening pleasure for San Rafael and all of Marin County.

This pen-and-ink drawing by a local artist depicts KTIM's studios and offices, which are in Heritage House in Victorian Village, San Rafael.

MARIN LIGHTS

In recent years a great deal has been learned about the art and science of lighting. Effective lighting can improve our performance in the work place, save us money in energy bills, and even alter our moods. Architects, interior designers, and do-it-yourself home decorators have discovered the enormous difference that attractive lighting can make in the overall decor of a home.

In 1960 two enlightened pioneers, Bill Everest and Herb Burford, foresaw the potential for lighting in future residential and commercial building trends. They also recognized the need for a lighting store in Marin County. There was only one other store in the area at the time, forcing many builders, electrical contractors, and consumers to shop for fixtures in San Francisco.

Both men were employed by an electrical specialty company in San Francisco, Everest as office manager and Burford as an outside salesman, and they figured that their "Mr. Inside, Mr. Outside" talents would complement each other perfectly. They were right; the company they founded together, Marin Lights, has survived and prospered for 27 years.

Opening at 658 Irwin Street, Marin Lights began as a small store, only 1,500 square feet. But, as Marin expanded in population in such new areas

as Terra Linda, Tiburon, and Greenbrae, so did the building trades. And with it came the need for expert home-lighting specialists.

By 1963 Marin Lights had doubled its original size, and in three years it had moved to a much larger facility across the street at 650 Irwin Street, the company's present location. Today Marin Lights occupies 16,000 square feet, including an elegant 4,000-square-foot showroom that displays a wide range of light fixtures, table lamps, floor lamps, mirrors, wall clocks, grandfather clocks, and other home furnishings. In 1979 Marin Lights of Santa Rosa opened to serve the needs of Sonoma County contractors and residents.

From the start Marin Lights was conceived as a full-service lighting center that offers personalized consulting to contractors and home owners alike, as well as a complete line of products from the world's leading manufacturers and from Marin Lights' own custom-designed line. The store's sales staff, trained in the technical aspects of lighting by the American Home Lighting Institute, are knowledgeable in all the latest home decorating trends and offer professional guidance for selecting fixtures in the planning stages, before building or remodeling actually

starts—the best time to make interior design decisions. The staff will even make house calls in order to find creative ways to make a large room warmer and cozier or a small room look larger.

This unique personalized approach has been a major reason for the company's success, as well as the partners' dedication to the business and their standing in the industry: Both Everest and Burford have held leadership positions in the Illuminating Engineers Society, Designers Lighting Forum, and the American Home Lighting Institute. In addition, Marin Lights contributes lighting to many community functions, such as school and local theater productions. The firm also acts as the primary lighting consultant for the Designer's Showcase, an annual renovation event in which local interior designers transform a San Rafael property into a dream home with the latest home decorating ideas.

For Marin Lights, the future certainly looks bright.

Established in San Rafael 27 years ago, Marin Lights now occupies this spacious facility at 650 Irwin Street. The elegant showroom displays a complete line of light fixtures, lamps, and home furnishings, including a variety of clocks.

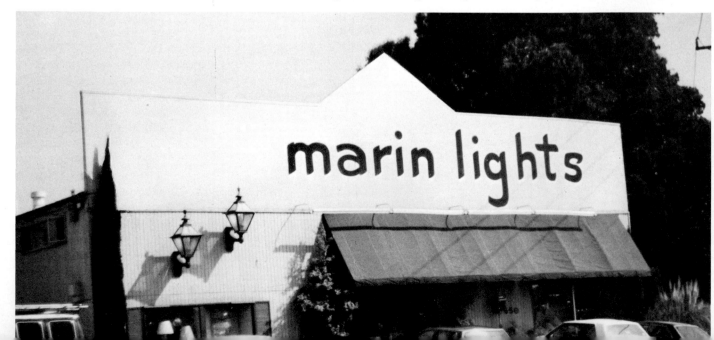

PATRONS

The following individuals, companies, and organizations have made a valuable commitment to the quality of this publication. Windsor Publications and the San Rafael Chamber of Commerce gratefully acknowledge their participation in *San Rafael: Marin's Mission City.*

Ace Printing & Mailing Service Inc.
Alphagraphics Printshops of the Future
An Affair to Remember Catering
    Company
Art Center
Anthony Bertotti Landscaping Inc.
Casa Marin Furniture
City of San Rafael*
Clarion Hotel Marin*
Cole Financial Group, Inc.*
    Kit M. Cole, President
    Bruce J. Baldwin, C.P.A.
    Franky Campbell
    Marcia Strand
    Terilynn Swanson
    Kimberly Alyson Tappan
    Catherine Tobin
Collins & Co.
The Edward N. DeMayo Family
Deming's Marin Tire and Brake
    Carlo's Transmission Service*
Dominic's Harbor Restaurant*
Jack A. Farley, Director-Marin Co.
    Historical Society
Earl Farnsworth Express*
Fireman's Fund*
Ghilotti Bros., Inc.*
House of Daniels, Black Point, Novato
Edwin G. Imhaus Company*
Kaiser Permanente*
Keaton Mortuaries
Klein TV & Electronics
KTIM AM/FM Radio*
The Mall at Northgate*
Margo and Beverly Margossian
Marin Advisors, Inc.
Marin Cleaners*
Marin General Hospital*
Marin Lights*
Marin Surplus*
Mount Tamalpais Cemetery and
    Mortuary*
New Horizons Savings and Loan
    Association*
Pacific Coast Title Co. of Marin

Paula's Florist
Phoenix American Incorporated*
Thelma H. Preston
Andrew James Ring III, AIA, Architect,
    Inc.*
St. Vincent's School for Boys
San Rafael Joe's*
San Rafael Redevelopment Agency
Shamrock Materials*
Silvestri & Hochman, Attorneys at Law
Stuber-Stroeh Associates, Inc.

*Partners in Progress of *San Rafael: Marin's Mission City.* The histories of these companies and organizations appear in Chapter 9, beginning on page 103.

*In commemoration of the 34 Marin County residents who fought
and died in World War I, a "Doughboy" statue was placed in front
of the Marin County Courthouse in San Rafael. When the Marin
County Civic Center was built close to today's Terra Linda, the
statue was moved to a nearby site. The plaque reads: "Erected by
the citizens of Marin County in memory of her sons who gave their
lives in the World War: 1917-1921." Courtesy, San Rafael Chamber of Commerce*

BIBLIOGRAPHY

Armentrout-Ma, L. Eve. "Chinese in California's Fishing Industry, 1850-1941." *California History.* Summer, 1981, pp. 142-157.

Arrigoni, Patricia. "San Rafael." *Making the Most of Marin. A California Guide.* Presidio Press, 1981, pp.131-167.

Bancroft, Hubert Howe. *The History of California.* 7 vols. San Francisco: The History Company, 1886.

Batman, Richard. *The Outer Coast.* San Diego, New York, London: Harcourt Brace Jovanovich, 1985.

Berger, John A. *The Franciscan missions of California.* Garden City, New York: Doubleday, 1948.

Cassady, Stephen. *Spanning the Gate.* Mill Valley, California: Squarebooks, 1979.

Chapman, Charles E. *A History of California. The Spanish Period.* New York: The MacMillan Co., 1925.

Cleaveland, Alice M. *The north bay shore during the Spanish and Mexican regimes.* M.A. thesis. University of California, Berkeley, 1932.

Cook, Sherbourne F. *The Conflict between the California Indian and the White Civilization.* Berkeley and Los Angeles: University of California Press, 1943.

Coy, Owen C. *A Pictorial History of California.* University of California Extension, Berkeley, 1925.

Davis, William H. *Seventy Five Years in California.* San Francisco: John Howell, 1929.

Dillon, Richard. *High Steel. Building the Bridge Across San Francisco Bay.* Millbrae, California: Celestial Arts, 1979.

Donnelly, Florence. "First the Mission, and then a village." *Independent Journal,* January 10, 1970.

Donnelly Florence. "San Rafael after the incorporation." *Independent Journal,* January 24, 1970.

Donnelly, Florence. "The people who made San Rafael." *Independent Journal,* January 31, 1970.

Donnelly, Florence. "People who made San Rafael." *Marin People.* Vol. I. Marin County Historical Society, 1971.

Donnelly, Florence G. *Early Days in Marin.* San Rafael: Marin County Savings and Loan Association. 3rd Printing, 1966.

Eldredge, Zoeth S. *The March of Portola and Discovery of the Bay of San Francisco.* San Francisco: California Promotion Committee, 1909.

Engelhardt, Zephyrin. *The Franciscans in California.* Harbor Springs, Michigan: Holy Childhood Indian School, 1897.

Farquhar, Francis P., ed. *Up and Down California in 1860-64. The Journal of William H. Brewer.* Berkeley and Los Angeles: University of California Press, 1949.

Fletcher, Francis. *The world encompassed by Sir Francis Drake being his next voyage to that to Nombre de Dios.* Printed for the Hakluyt Society, 1854.

Galvin, John, ed. *The First Spanish Entry into San Francisco Bay, 1775.* San Francisco: John Howell Books, 1921.

Gardner, Dorothy. "The First Settlers of San Rafael." *Independent Journal,* May 4, 1974.

Gardner, Dorothy. "Early San Rafael recalled." *Independent Journal,* May 25, 1974.

Gift, George W. *Something about California.* San Rafael: San Rafael Herald, 1875.

Gilliam, Harold. "Marin's Proudest Man-Made Monument." *Image of Marin.* First Annual Edition, 1966, pp. 36-39.

Golden Gate Bridge Fiesta. Official Program San Francisco, May 27-June 2, 1937.

The Golden Gate Bridge. Report of the Chief Engineer (Joseph B. Strauss). September, 1937.

Hanna, Phil Townsend. *California Through Four Centuries. A Handbook of Memorable Historical Dates.* New York: Farrar & Rhinehart, 1935.

Hanna, Warren L. *Lost Harbor. The Controversy over Drake's California Anchorage.* Berkeley: University of California Press, 1979.

Heizer, R.F., and Whipple, M.A., eds. *The California Indians. A Source Book.* Second Edition. Berkeley: University of California Press, 1971.

Heizer, Robert F. *Francis Drake and the California Indians, 1579.* University of California Press, 1947.

Heizer, Robert F. *Elizabethan California.* Ramona, California: Ballena Press, 1974.

Heizer, Robert F. "Archeological Evidence of Sebastian Rodriguez Cermenho's California Visit in 1595." *California Historical Society Quarterly.* Vol. XX, No. 4, December, 1941.

Heizer, Robert F., and Kroeber, Theodore. *Ishi the Last Yahi. A Documentary History.* Berkeley: University of California Press, 1979.

Hittell, Theodore H. *History of California.* 4 vols. San Francisco: N.J. Stone, 1885-1897.

Holliday, J.S. *The World Rushed In. The California Gold Rush Experience.* New York: Simon & Schuster, 1981.

Hussey, John A. *Mission San Rafael Arcangel.* Berkeley: Works Progress Administration, 1936.

Kotzebue, Otto von. *A new voyage round the world, in the years 1823, 24, 25 and 26.* 2 vols. London: Henry Colburn and Richard Bentley, 1830.

Kroeber, Alfred L. *Handbook of the Indians of California.* Washington D.C. Government Printing Office, 1925.

Kroeber, Theodora. *Ishi in Two Worlds. A Biography of the Last Wild Indian in North America.* Berkeley: University of California Press, 1962.

LeBaron, Gaye. *Santa Rosa, A Nineteenth Century Town.* Santa Rosa, California: Historia Ltd., 1985.

McKittrick, Myrtle M. *Vallejo, Son of California.* Portland, Oregon: Binfords & Mort, 1944.

Marin County Historical Society Bulletins: Vols. I through XIII (1967-1980).

Marin County Journal. Illustrated Edition. October, 1887.

The Marin Journal. New Era Edition. San Rafael, Marin County, California, 1909.

Marin People. Vol. I (1971), Vol. II (1972), Vol III (1980). Marin County Historical Society.

Marinship. The History of a Wartime Shipyard. San Francisco: 1947.

Mason, Jack, with Van Cleave Park, Helen. *Early Marin.* Written under the auspices of the Marin Historical Society. Petaluma, California: House of Printing, 1971.

Mason, Jack, with Van Cleave Park, Helen. *The Making of Marin (1850-1975).* Written under the auspices of the Marin County Historical Society. Inverness, California: North Shore Books, 1975.

Mathes, Michael W. *Vizcaino and Spanish Expansion in the Pacific Ocean, 1580-1630.* San Francisco: California Historical Society, 1968.

Meret, Charles O. *Chronological History of Marin County: 1542-1936.* 3 vols. Typescript.

Miller, Crane S., and Hyslop, Richard S. *California. The Geography of Diversity.* Palo Alto, California: Mayfield Publishing Co., 1983.

Munro-Fraser, J.P. *History of Marin County.* San Francisco: Alley, Bowen and Co., 1880.

Oakeshott, Gordon B. *California's Changing Landscapes. A Guide to the Geology of the State.* McGraw Hill, 1978.

Old Marin With Love. Published by the Marin County American Revolution Bicentennial Commission, 1976.

Olmstead, S.H. "San Rafael, the Beautiful." *Overland Monthly.* October, 1908.

Pitt, Leonard. *California Controversies. Major Issues in the History of the State.* San Rafael: ETRI Publishing Company, 1985.

Powers, Stephen. *Tribes of California.* Berkeley: University of California Press, 1976.

Priestly, Herbert Ingram. *Franciscan Explorations in California: Spain in the West.* Vol. VI. Glendale, California: Arthur H. Clarke, 1946.

Quinn, Arthur. *Broken Shore: The Marin Peninsula—A Perspective on History.* Salt Lake City: Peregrine Smith, 1981.

Radford, Dr. Evelyn Morris. *The Bridge and the Building. The art of government and the government of Art.* New York: Carlton Press, 1973.

"Reminiscences of Charles Lauff." *San Rafael Independent Journal.* January 23-May 23, 1916.

Richardson, Stephen J. *The days of the dons, reminiscences of California's oldest native.* San Francisco Call Bulletin, 1918.

Roske, Ralph J. *Everyman's Eden. A History of California.* New York: MacMillan Co., 1968.

Rothwell, Bertha Stedman. *Pioneering in Marin County. A Historical Recording.* Typescript, 1959.

Royce, Josiah. *California. A Study of American Character.* New York: Alfred A. Knopf, 1948.

San Rafael illustrated and described showing its advantages for homes. San Francisco: W.W. Elliott, 1884.

Scherer, James A.B. *The Lion of the Vigilantes, William T. Coleman.* Bobbs-Merrill Co., 1939.

Slaymaker, Charles M. *Cry for Olompali.* An Initial Report on the Archeological and Historical Features of Olompali. October, 1972.

Spencer-Hancock, Diane, and Pritchard, William E. "The Chapel at Fort Ross, Its History and Reconstruction." *California History.* Spring, 1982, pp. 3-17.

Vanderbilt, Major Newell. "History of Marin County," pp. 441-479 in Ira B. Cross' *Financing an Empire. History of Banking in California.* Chicago, San Francisco, Los Angeles: S.J. Clarke, 1927.

van der Zee, John. *The Gate. The True Story of the Design and Construction of the Golden Gate Bridge.* New York: Simon and Schuster, 1986.

Weber, Msgr. Francis J., ed. *The Penultimate Mission. A documentary history of San Rafael, Arcangel.* Hong Kong: Libra Press Limited, 1983.

INDEX

2 YEARS OLD

S. QUENTIN POINT LANDING.

SA